# FOCUSING ON
# IELTS

## LISTENING
## AND
## SPEAKING
## SKILLS

## Kerry O'Sullivan
## and
## Steven Thurlow

National Centre for English Language Teaching and Research

# Contents

**TRANSCRIPTS**

## Unit 1: Listening

## Unit 2: Speaking

**ANSWER KEY**

# Acknowledgments

We would like to thank the following people for their personal and professional support throughout the writing of this book: James George, Mavis O'Sullivan, Martin Sitompul, Judge Helen O'Sullivan, Lyn Mickelborough and Werner Borkhardt.

We would also like to thank Mary Jane Hogan, Alex Barthel and Michael Carey for their professional advice and comments on the 'tricky bits' of the manuscript.

Thanks are also due to the teachers and students at English Language Services, NCELTR, who trialled material from the book or lent their voices when needed. Special thanks go to Mark Brown, Claire Hicklin, Pattama Patpong, Lorraine Sorrell and the always inspirational Sharynne Wade.

Assistance also came from elsewhere in NCELTR. Thanks to Frances, Jo, Nanette and Prue in the Resources Centre, Madeleine and Valerie in the Independent Learning Centre and Helen, Kris and Muammer in the Publications Unit. Finally, a special thank you to Louise Melov for her support throughout the whole project.

Kerry O'Sullivan
Steven Thurlow

# How to use this book

You can use this book individually as an independent-study book to prepare you for the IELTS test or as a coursebook in an IELTS preparation course with a teacher. Both sections of the book are for General Training and Academic candidates.

Passages marked **READ ME** give you information about language skills, with **EXAMPLES** to follow and **EXERCISES** for you to do.

You should read and study the book from the beginning to the end. Do Unit 1: Listening and then Unit 2: Speaking.

Both Unit 1: Listening and Unit 2: Speaking contain the following six sections.

**1   What is in the module?**

The first section gives a description of the IELTS test, with information about what it contains, how long it is, what kinds of questions there are, and so on. You should read this section in conjunction with the IELTS Handbook that you receive when you register for the IELTS test.

**2   Test-taking tips**

The section gives you test-taking tips, advice to help you complete the test within the time allowed and to help you carry out the test in ways that will give you the best mark possible.

**3   The strategies you need**

The section on strategies gives you advice and some practice on how to listen and speak as effectively and efficiently as possible when you do the IELTS test.

**4   The skills you need**

This is the main section of each unit because it explains and practises the skills that you need to do well in the Listening and Speaking Modules. These skills include understanding what is said, the different types of information and what listeners are doing; speaking fluently and accurately; and using vocabulary and stress appropriately. There are a number of short exercises to help you develop these skills. You should do these exercises without assistance and you should follow any time limits suggested. The answers to the exercises are at the back of the book.

**5   Developing your study program**

This section helps you develop your own regular self-study program. This involves deciding your needs, finding appropriate practice materials, and practising your skills. There are exercises suggested for individual study and exercises that you can do with a study partner.

**6   IELTS practice tests**

These practice tests are designed to be similar to actual IELTS tests. You should do these practice tests without any assistance and you should follow the time limits given.

# Summary of exercises

This list gives the aim of each exercise and where you can find it.

## Unit 1: Listening

## Unit 2: Speaking

# FOCUSING ON
# IELTS

## LISTENING AND SPEAKING SKILLS

# UNIT 1: Listening

# 1 What is in the IELTS listening module?

| | Academic and General Training candidates<br>All candidates do the same listening test. |
|---|---|
| **Time allowed** | 30 minutes |
| **Procedure** | The listening module (test) is the first module you will do when you take the IELTS.<br><br>The listening module is recorded on a tape which is played in the examination room. The tape is played only once, without pause.<br><br>Candidates are given a question paper. As they listen to the tape, they write their answers on the question paper.<br><br>When the tape ends, candidates are given 10 minutes to transfer their answers to an answer sheet. |
| **Number of questions** | A total of 40 questions in four sections<br>(usually 10 questions per section) |
| **Format of questions** | (See examples of types of questions in<br>Unit 2: Test-taking tips in this book) |
| **Structure of test** | Section 1: A conversation between two speakers about a social/semi-official topic<br><br>Section 2: A monologue (ie spoken by one speaker) about a social (non-academic) topic<br><br>Section 3: A conversation between two to four speakers about an academic topic<br><br>Section 4: A university-style presentation by one speaker about an academic topic<br><br>Sometimes a section may be spread over two to three pages of the question paper. |

# 2 Test-taking tips

What should you do when you take the IELTS listening module? Here are some suggestions about how to manage the test-taking as well as possible.

### BE PREPARED

**READ ME**

Make sure you arrive at the examination centre early so that you are relaxed and calm when the test begins. Dress comfortably. Bring at least two pens and two pencils.

> **Remember: The Listening Test comes first.**

### KEEP YOUR EYES ON THE PAPER AND YOUR EARS ON THE TAPE

**READ ME**

One of the main challenges of the IELTS Listening Test is that you must do three things more or less at the same time:

- Listen
- Read
- Write.

To achieve this, you need to concentrate and manage yourself very carefully. Throughout the test, keep your eyes on the question paper (so that you can read the questions and write your answers) and keep your ears carefully fixed on the tape (so that you can hear what the speakers are saying). There is no point in looking up at the tape – and it will reduce your ability to concentrate on reading the questions and writing the answers.

You need to practise listening to people *without seeing them*. You can do this by listening to a radio, a cassette, or a television while you read. It is a good idea to try to visualise the people as they speak. Also, it would be useful to practise this type of highly-focused listening while there are some distractions (for example, other people coughing or moving their chairs, or with some noises from outside the room).

### GUESS

**READ ME**

Try to answer all the questions. If necessary, *guess* the answer. There are no penalties for wrong answers. Complete all your answers at the end of each section – don't wait until the end of the test. It will be more difficult to select/guess answers then.

### MANAGE YOUR TIME

**READ ME**

Doing the IELTS Listening Test requires careful time management and self-discipline.

You will hear the tape only once. If you cannot answer a question, don't become stuck on it. Choose an answer, and then move on when the instructions on the tape tell you to.

You are given time to read each set of questions before the tape is played. Use this time well to decide what kind of information is needed to answer each question (see Section 3 'The listening strategies you need' for some practice in doing this).

You are given some time to review each set of answers. Use this time fully, and don't be tempted to look ahead at the next section.

Throughout the test don't waste time by erasing or using 'white-out': just draw a line through the word you want to change and keep going.

## WRITE ACCURATELY

READ ME

Although this is a listening test, your ability to *write* accurate answers is also relevant. Both incorrect grammar and spelling in your answers are penalised. At the end of the test you are given 10 minutes to transfer your answers from the question paper to the answer sheet. Make sure you transfer all your answers completely and accurately. As you transfer, check whether your grammar is correct (eg should this noun be singular or plural?). Also check your spelling. You can cross out and change your answers – untidiness is not penalised, as long as your writing can be clearly understood.

## KNOW WHAT TO EXPECT

READ ME

It is important to know what to expect in the Listening Test. Make sure that you are thoroughly familiar with the structure and layout of the test.

Remember that the test becomes more difficult as you move from Section 1 to Section 4. Expect this, and stay calm.

It is also important to know how the tape will instruct you during the test.

At the beginning of each section of the Listening Test, the speaker on the tape gives a brief introduction to the situation:

> You are now going to listen to a conversation in a computer shop. Martin is looking at computers and talking to a woman working in the shop.

Remember – you hear this, but you do not see it on the question paper.

The speaker then gives instructions:

> Read questions 1 to 5. As you listen to the tape, write the correct answer in the spaces provided.

The speaker then tells you to look at the questions:

> First you have some time to look at questions 1 to 5.

Then the tape is silent for 30 seconds to give you time to read the questions carefully. After 30 seconds, the speaker then repeats which questions you have to answer:

> Now listen and answer questions 1 to 5.

Then the situation will be played.

To become familiar with how instructions are given in an IELTS Listening Test, you should do as many practice tests as possible. There is an IELTS practice test in Unit 1: 6 of this book.

Make sure that you familiarise yourself with the different types of questions in the Listening Test. *The IELTS Handbook* states that a variety of questions are used, chosen from the following types:

- multiple-choice questions
- short-answer questions
- sentence completion
- notes/summary/diagram/flow chart/table completion
- labelling a diagram
- classification
- matching.

**EXAMPLES**

The following are examples of the different question types you may encounter in the Listening Test. Listen to the tape and answer questions 1 to 16.

**Multiple choice questions**

Questions 1 and 2

Circle the correct letters **A**, **B** or **C**.

**1** Which shop is Martin in?

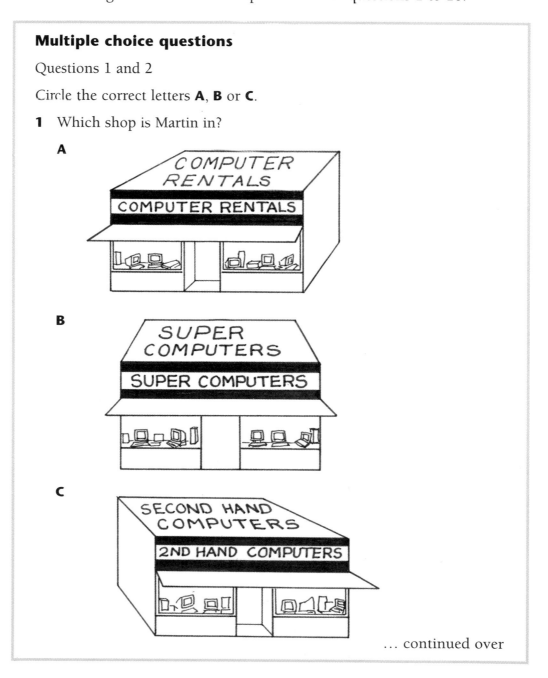

... continued over

... continued

**2** Martin wants to get ...

    **A** a laptop computer

    **B** a desktop computer

    **C** a palmtop computer

## Short-answer questions

Questions 3 and 4

Write NO MORE THAN THREE WORDS for each answer.

**3** What type of computer does the shop sell most of? _____

**4** What will Martin mainly use the computer for? _____

## Sentence completion

Questions 5 and 6

Write NO MORE THAN THREE WORDS for each answer.

Light laptops are usually (**5**) _____ than heavy laptops.

The Apex is the most expensive because it is the (**6**) _____.

## Notes/summary/diagram/flow chart/table completion

Questions 7 and 8

Complete the notes.

| <u>Apex</u> | <u>Sunray</u> | <u>Nu-tech</u> |
| --- | --- | --- |
| 1.9 kg | _____(**7**) | 3.1 kg |
| most convenient | _____(**8**) | cheapest |

## Labelling a diagram which has numbered parts

Questions 9 and 10

Complete the diagram.

Write NO MORE THAN THREE WORDS for each answer.

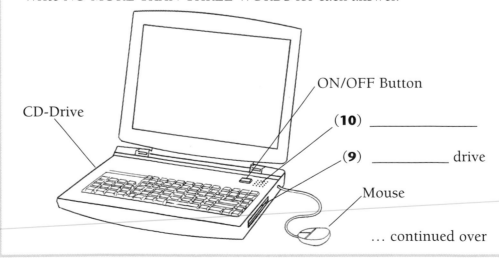

CD-Drive

ON/OFF Button

(**10**) _____

(**9**) _____ drive

Mouse

... continued over

... continued

## Classification

Questions 11 to 13

Complete the table showing the types of pointing devices used by different computers.

| M | = | **M**ouse |
|---|---|---|
| T | = | **T**ouchpad |
| TB | = | **T**rack **B**all |

| | Sunray laptop | Apex laptop | Nu-tech laptop |
|---|---|---|---|
| **Type of pointing device** | 11 | 12 | 13 |

## Matching

Questions 14 to 16

Match the computers in questions 14 to 16 with the appropriate labels **A**, **B** or **C**.

**14** Apex _____

**15** Sunray _____

**16** Nu-tech _____

| A | B | C |
|---|---|---|
| 12 MONTHS PARTS ONLY 12 GUARANTEE | 6 MONTHS PARTS ONLY GUARANTEE | 12 MONTHS 12 PARTS AND LABOUR GUARANTEE |

# 3 The listening strategies you need

Here are three important strategies to use when you are doing the Listening Test. They will help you to approach the test in the right way.

- Be ready to listen for the specific information you need to answer the question.

- Focus on more than one question at a time while you are listening.

- Match what you see on the question paper with what you hear on the tape.

## LISTENING FOR SPECIFIC INFORMATION

**READ ME**

It is not necessary to comprehend *every* word of the passages in the Listening Test. Of course, you will listen *to* every word in the passage, but you don't need to listen *for* every word.

What is the difference between 'listening *to*' something and 'listening *for*' something?

| Listening _to_ something | You hear it. You receive it in your ears. |
|---|---|
| Listening _for_ something | You are waiting to hear something. You are ready to catch a specific piece of information. You are listening actively. |

You only need to listen *for* the specific information which answers the question. The strategy of listening for specific information is similar to 'scanning' when you are reading [see *Focusing on IELTS: Reading and writing skills;* page 7]. You focus on catching a particular piece of information, not on all of the information.

## Predicting

The key to listening for specific information is predicting the type of information that you need to listen for.

You read the following question on the question paper:

Why did Martin leave work early?

Before you hear the tape you can predict that there will be a reason given, using words like *because* or *so*, and perhaps giving information about being ill or having an appointment or being tired.

It is important to make good use of the 30 seconds of silence which the tape gives you for each set of questions (*First you have some time to look at questions x to y*). As quickly as possible, read the questions and decide what kind of information you will listen for.

Use the same strategy for multiple-choice questions. During your preparation time, identify the differences in the answers, and decide what to listen for.

**EXAMPLE**

How many Canadian speakers will attend the conference?

   **A** 20

   **B** 30

   **C** 25

Here you need to be ready to listen for just one piece of information (a number). When the tape plays, you expect to hear something like: 'There will be (*number*) Canadian speakers at the conference'.

Sometimes you need to listen for two pieces of information.

**EXAMPLE**      What type of accommodation does he rent?

    **A**  a two-bedroom house

    **B**  a one-bedroom apartment

    **C**  a three-bedroom apartment

You can see that the answers differ in two ways. So you are listening for two pieces of information: (1) Is it a house or an apartment? (2) How many bedrooms does it have?

 **2**

---

### Exercise 1: Listening for specific information

What would you listen *for* if you saw the following questions? Predict the type of information needed. One has been done for you as an example.

| | **Information needed** | **Answers** |
|---|---|---|
| **1** When is Sue going to finish her assignment | *a time/a day* | |
| **2** Why did Sue enjoy the assignment? | | |
| **3** What proportion of university students are female? | | |
| **4** How many women Vice-Chancellors are there? | | |
| **5** What part of Sue's assignment remains unfinished? | | |

Now listen to the tape and answer the questions.

---

## Underlining/highlighting key question words

**READ ME**      When you read the questions, underline or highlight the key words. The key words ask for the information. This means that 'wh-' words and nouns are usually key words, whereas words like 'and', 'of', 'the', 'did' and 'so' are usually not key words.

**EXAMPLE**      <u>Where</u> is the <u>computer</u>?

    <u>What</u> is the <u>advantage</u> of using <u>solar power</u>?

    <u>What</u> are the <u>two main causes</u> of an <u>ageing population</u>?

    <u>When</u> will the <u>conference begin</u>?

**3**

## Exercise 2: Listening for specific information

Take 30 seconds to look at the questions, underline the key words, and get ready to listen to the tape.

**1** At what time did the robbery take place? _____

**2** What is the name of the bank which was robbed? _____

**3** How many customers were in the bank at the time of the robbery? _____

**4** How many people were involved in robbing the bank? _____

**5** What telephone number should people call to give information? _____

Now listen to the tape and answer the questions.

Write NO MORE THAN THREE WORDS for each answer.

## Changing pictures into words

**READ ME**
You also need to decide what to listen for when the question contains pictures. During the 30 seconds you have to study the questions, you can turn the pictures into words. Quickly locate different details in the pictures and express them in words in your mind. Then you can listen for those words when the tape is played.

**EXAMPLE**

Who is the new lecturer?

You are ready to listen for two details: (1) Is the person a man or woman? and (2) Is the person short or tall? Then, when you listen to the tape and hear 'her' and 'she' and 'tall', you know that the correct answer is C.

## Exercise 3a: Listening for specific information

Look at the pictures and quickly decide what to listen for.

What kind of visa did Helen get?

**A**

**B**

**C**

**READ ME** Now you are ready to answer the question. You know what you will be listening for (eg I'm listening for the *type* of visa and *for how long*). So, if you hear information about the *cost* of the visa or the *conditions* of the visa, you know you don't have to be concerned with it. It is not relevant so you can ignore it. Sometimes when you are listening you must ignore quite large sections of irrelevant information. Stay calm and keep waiting. Keep listening for the information you need.

**5**

---

### Exercise 3b: Listening for specific information

Now listen to the tape and answer the question.

---

**READ ME** The strategy of predicting what information you need to listen for in order to answer questions and then actively listening for that specific information applies to all sections of the Listening Test and to all types of questions. In the following exercise you can practise the strategy while doing a 'notes-completion' question type.

 **6**

---

### Exercise 4: Listening for specific information

**1** Look at the following questions and quickly decide what to listen for in order to answer them.

Questions 1 to 4

Complete the notes below. Write NO MORE THAN THREE WORDS for each answer.

> ESSAY
>
> Topic:       Attitudes towards public transport
>
> Length:       **(1)** _____
>
> **(2)** _____   open (eg telephone survey)
>
>                         face-to-face interviews
>
>                         case study
>
> Due date:       **(3)** _____
>
> Requirements:     word processed
>
>                       **(4)** _____
>
>                         description of methodology

**2** Now listen to the tape and answer the questions.

For more practice in using this strategy, see Unit 1: 5.

## FOCUSING ON MORE THAN ONE QUESTION

**READ ME** The second strategy you need to develop in order to do well in the Listening Test is an extension of the first strategy (listening for specific information). It is necessary because the tape tells you when to move on to the next section, but it does not tell you when to move on to the next question *within* each section. For example, if you are doing a gap-filling task, the speaker on the tape does not tell you that you have already heard the information for gap number 3 and should now move on to gap number 4. You have to decide this for yourself. If you focus only on gap number 3, you may miss the information that will help you to answer the next question (gap number 4). You may lose your place entirely and panic. To prevent this happening, you need to focus on more than one question at all times. That is, you need to listen at the same time for information to answer at least two questions.

**EXAMPLE**          On your question paper you see the following:

Flight number:          (**1**) _____

Departure time:         (**2**) _____

Cost of ticket:         (**3**) _____

Cost of departure tax:  (**4**) _____

As you listen to the tape, you need to focus on at least two questions at a time. You will need to work something like this:

1   You think: 'I'm listening for a flight number and a time'.

2   After you catch and fill in question (1), you then think 'I'm listening for a time and a cost'.

3   After you catch the time and fill in answer (2), you say to yourself 'I'm listening for the cost of the ticket and the cost of the tax', and so on.

Sometimes it is possible to group the questions by topic (eg (3) and (4): 'I'm listening for two costs'). Underlining the key words during the time you have to read the questions will help you to listen for several questions at once. (See 'Underlining/highlighting key question words' above.)

 7

---

### Exercise 5: Focusing on more than one question

Mia is telephoning an airline company. Listen to the conversation and answer the questions. Write NO MORE THAN THREE WORDS for each answer.

1   What is Mia's flight number?                                       _____

2   For what date is Mia's original flight reservation?               _____

3   How many times per week does Sky Air fly direct to Honolulu?      _____

4   Where does Mia want to sit?                                        _____

5   How many kilos of luggage is Mia allowed to take on the flight?   _____

6   What will Mia have to do if her luggage is too heavy?             _____

7   Did Mia achieve the main things she wanted to in her telephone call? _____

---

**READ ME**          It is important to understand that the sequence of information on the tape is always the same as the sequence of questions. This helps you to follow (and answer) the questions in the right order.

Sometimes the information you need to answer a question is presented more than once by the speaker(s). This gives you a chance to select the correct answer and then confirm your selection. For example, if you check the transcript for Exercise 5, you will see that the information you need to answer question 2 (the flight number) is given twice in the dialogue. When the information is repeated at a later point you can go back to question 2 and select your answer or confirm your selection.

Some questions require you to listen for information that is presented over a large section of the passage. For example, in Exercise 5 the information you need to answer question 7 is spread throughout the dialogue. You need to consider most of the dialogue in order to answer the question.

Exercise 5 is an example of an IELTS Section 1-type task.

> **Please note that the strategy of focusing on more than one question at a time is necessary in all sections of the test.**

In the following exercise you can practise the strategy in a 'diagram-completion' question.

 **8**

---

**Exercise 6: Focusing on more than one question**

Questions 1 to 4

Complete the diagram.

Write NO MORE THAN THREE WORDS for each answer.

```
┌─────────────────────────────────────┐
│   Ace Security Alarm System          │────(1) _____
│   ┌─────────────────────────┐        │
│   │      DISARMED            │────────│──Activate
│   │      READY TO ARM        │────────│
│   └─────────────────────────┘        │
│                                       │────(2) _____
│   Off   Away  Reset  Function         │
│   □     □     □      □      □  C──────│
│                                       │────(3) _____
│   □     □     □      □      □  *      │
│                                       │────(4) _____
│   For emergencies, phone 13 80 00    │
└─────────────────────────────────────┘
```

For more practice in using this strategy, see Unit 1: 5.

---

## MATCHING THE MEANING

**READ ME**  Often in the listening test you must match what you see on the question paper with what you hear on the tape. Sometimes it is easy to find the match because you hear exactly the same words as you see.

**EXAMPLE**

| You see this question on the question paper: | You hear this sentence on the tape: |
| --- | --- |
| Why didn't he go back to university? | *I didn't have enough money.* |

**A** he wanted to get a job

**B** he didn't have enough money

**C** he had already earned enough money

Clearly, the answer is B because the words match exactly. Often, however, you will not hear the exact words; instead you will hear the same *meaning*.

**EXAMPLE**

You see this question on the question paper:

Why didn't he go back to university?

**A** he wanted to get a job

**B** he couldn't afford it

**C** he had already earned enough money

You hear this sentence on the tape:

*I didn't have enough money.*

Answer B is correct. Although it uses words which are different from the tape, it has the same meaning. You need to match the meaning, not just match the words. Knowing synonyms (words with the same meaning, eg help/assist, enough/sufficient, finish/complete, can't afford/don't have enough money) will help you to match the meaning. Learning synonyms is an important part of vocabulary learning – especially at an advanced level of English (see Unit 1: 4).

 9

---

### Exercise 7: Matching the meaning

Questions 1 to 4

Circle the correct letter **A**, **B** or **C**.

**1** Swimmers wear full-length swimsuits because:

  **A** they like the way the swimsuits look.

  **B** this is required in competitive swimming.

  **C** they enhance swimmers' performance.

**2** The experiments in 1990 showed that shaving body hair:

  **A** helps swimmers to swim faster.

  **B** lowers swimmers' consumption of oxygen.

  **C** reduces drag by around 10%.

**3** The new-style swimsuits:

  **A** resemble shark skin.

  **B** are made of shark skin.

  **C** are covered with shark skin.

**4** Sharks are able to swim so fast because:

  **A** their skin is very smooth.

  **B** their skin has very small ridges.

  **C** their skin has survived for a long time.

---

Exercise 7 is an example of an IELTS Section 4-type task.

**The strategy of matching meaning is necessary in all sections of the test and with all question types.**

**READ ME**

Note that the matching of meaning is not always direct. The item on the question paper may be an inference; that is, a conclusion based on the evidence available. In the following exercise, for example, you are asked to draw conclusions about the speakers' views. Although the speakers do not necessarily express their views directly (such as 'I support this idea' or 'I am in favour of that proposal'), it is nevertheless possible to draw inferences about their views. The evidence includes tone of voice (eg very enthusiastic or very dismissive) and the words they use (eg 'I think that's ridiculous').

 **10**

---

**Exercise 8: Matching the meaning**

**1** Which students support the idea of requiring politicians to have a university degree?

_____

**2** Which students are in favour of a minimum age requirement for political candidates?

_____

For more practice in matching meaning, see Unit 1: 5.

---

# 4 The listening skills you need

To be a good listener you need to develop a range of skills which we can broadly describe as 'understanding what speakers are saying' and 'understanding what speakers are doing'. These two sets of skills complement each other and a successful listener is skillful in both areas. In this section we will deal with these two sets of skills one-by-one.

## UNDERSTANDING WHAT SPEAKERS ARE SAYING

**READ ME**

To be able to understand what speakers are saying you need to be able to:

- recognise their pronunciation
- understand the vocabulary they use
- guess the meaning of unfamiliar words reasonably accurately.

## Recognising meaning through pronunciation

The speakers on the listening tape of the IELTS Listening Test generally have standard British, Australian, New Zealand, or North American accents. They speak quite clearly and at a speed that is slightly less than normal. However, if you are not used to listening to English their speed of speaking may seem very fast. The speakers on the cassette accompanying this book speak in a similar manner to those in the IELTS Listening Test.

We will now discuss and practise four specific listening skills you need to develop in order to understand what people are saying in the Listening Test and in real life. These are an ablity to:

- recognise words
- recognise content words
- catch the sentence focus
- understand the status of information.

For further examples, explanation, and practice in these four skills see *In tempo: An English pronunciation course* by Halina Zawadski (NCELTR, 1994).

## Recognising words

Sometimes you may fail to recognise familiar words when spoken by English speakers. There are a number of possible reasons for this:

- English speakers do not pronounce all the syllables of words equally clearly and strongly. They give main (primary) stress to only one of the syllables in each word (eg the main stress in 'international' is on the third of its five syllables, namely in ter <u>NA</u> tion al).

- Native speakers often 'contract' (shorten) words when they speak (eg *It will stop* contracts to *It'll stop* and *did not go* to *didn't go*). In informal speech, contraction is common and sometimes the word almost disappears completely (eg in *Have you seen it?* the beginning of the 'have' may disappear, and the 'v' may join the 'you' so that it sounds like *'Vyou seen it'*)?

- Native speakers often reduce unstressed or weak syllables to a very short sound that is commonly called the 'schwa'. This sound /ə/ is found in the first syllable of words such as 'ago' and 'o'clock' and the last syllable of 'teacher' and 'centre'. The 'schwa' is the most common of all sounds in English.

- When some sounds occur side by side, they may change. For example, in 'Did you go?' the second 'd' joins the 'y' to create a new 'j' sound, resulting in 'Di-jou go?'

 11

### Exercise 9: Recognising words (Dictogloss)

Listen to a short passage as it is read at normal speed three times. The first time it is read simply listen. The second and third times copy down as many words as you can.

As the train _____

_____

_____

_____

Now compare your version with the one in the Answer key.

**READ ME**
Exercise 9 should have demonstrated how difficult it is to 'pick up' every word when listening to a talk in English. Think about the words you heard clearly. What sort of words were they? What about the words you missed? Were they important in your final understanding of the passage? Did you miss some words because they were reduced or contracted? Did you hear any schwas?

Turn to Exercise 39 in Unit 2 for more information on word stress in the context of the IELTS Speaking Test.

### Recognising content words

We have seen that English speakers stress some words when they speak and leave others unstressed. They strongly stress 'content words' – that is, words which give new information to the listener – and leave other words, those that join the information words together, unstressed or weak. For example look at the sentence:

<u>Tea</u> is one of the most <u>popular</u> drinks in the <u>world</u>.

The three most important words that communicate meaning in this sentence are stressed.

**12**

---

## Exercise 10: Recognising content words

Listen to the following talk on travel writing. Underline the words you predict the speaker will probably stress to communicate the main information. Then listen to the tape to check whether your predictions were correct. The first sentence has been done for you as an example.

The <u>last</u> decade of the <u>twentieth</u> <u>century</u> witnessed an <u>explosion</u> of <u>interest</u> in the field of <u>travel</u> <u>writing</u>. Bookshops that once had shelves stocked only with atlases, guidebooks and maps now include sections devoted to narrative and other personal accounts of travel. So why the massive growth in this type of travel writing? Some would give credit to a number of authors who have re-invigorated travel writing, with readers enthusiastically responding to their entertaining and often humorous style. But to my mind, the main aim of travel writing is to break the barrier of print and time and to make destinations alive in the mind of the reader.

Now check your answers in the Answer key.

---

## Catching the focus

**READ ME**     English speakers frequently use a very strong 'focus stress' to show what part of their message they want their listeners to focus on. For example:

**EXAMPLES**         A:  Professor, can I talk to you about my research project?

          B:  Let's talk about your <u>essay</u> first.

Sometimes English speakers give a word focus stress in order to correct the listener's comprehension mistakes, or to contrast information. For example:

    No, I didn't go to <u>Liverpool</u>. I went to <u>Newcastle</u>.

In the IELTS Listening Test, focus stress can help you to predict where the answers might be, as key information to answer questions is usually presented with strong focus stress.

 **13**

---

## Exercise 11: Catching the focus

Listen to the final part of the talk on travel writing. Predict the words the speaker will focus on and underline them. Why does he particularly stress these words?

So, I ask again, why this growth in travel writing? Is it because of these wonderful authors who have re-invented a tired genre? Or is it another reason? I would explain the popularity of the new travel writing as caused by the ever-expanding sameness and uniformity of the world. Nowadays, people find it harder and harder even to find, let alone travel to unusual places themselves, so they want to read about others doing it. Or, if the writing is about a familiar place, they may want to read how it's been given a new or unusual twist by a talented author.

Now check your answers in the Answer key.

---

Turn to Exercises 40 and 41 in Unit 2 for more information on focus stress in the context of the IELTS Speaking Test.

## Understanding the status of information

**READ ME**  Listening to a person's intonation (ie the rising/high/low/falling tone of their voice) can help you understand the status or role of the information that the speaker is giving. If the information given is main information, a rising or high tone ( ⟋ ) is used. If the information is additional, or a comment on the main information, a falling or low tone is used ( ⟍ ). In the IELTS Listening Test, intonation can help you predict where the answers might be.

**14**

**EXAMPLE**  Listen to the example on the tape:

This year I'm studying CHEMistry – in fact I've

just bought the main textbook – and PHYsics.

---

### Exercise 12: Predicting main and additional information from intonation

Listen to an excerpt from a lecture on educational multimedia. As you listen, pay particular attention to the intonation the speaker has used and indicate what is important or main information by adding directional arrows to the relevant parts of the sentence. The first two sentences have been done for you as an example.

Good morning class. Today, I'd like to talk about producing educational multimedia.

This particular type of multimedia – as distinct from entertainment multimedia – is an area

of interest for educators everywhere. I'd particularly like to discuss the process of producing

this type of multimedia. Your first consideration, apart from deciding what medium you're

going to deliver your product through, is your audience. Who they are, what they expect

and, most importantly, what they need. After you have determined this basic information

about your users, then you can go on to the all important area of content.

Now check your answers in the Answer key.

---

**READ ME**  Attention to intonation can help you in the IELTS Listening Test to predict what is coming next in a talk. Specifically, it can help you determine what is finished and unfinished information. If a speaker is about to finish giving information, their intonation will rise and then fall sharply, but if the information is unfinished, with more to come, the intonation will be steady with a low rise.

**15**

**EXAMPLE**  Listen to the example on the tape as the speaker lists things, using intonation to indicate if she has finished her list:

I think we're ready. We've got pens, pencils, erasers, and a stapler.

## Exercise 13: Predicting completeness of information from intonation

Listen to the intonation in the following sentences and determine whether the information is complete or not. As you listen, write **C** for Complete or **I** for Incomplete next to the sentences. The first sentence has been done for you as an example.

**1**  Cacti are part of a group of plants called succulents.      <u>  I  </u>

**2**  I'd like you to meet my friend, Vanessa.      <u>     </u>

**3**  We have a wide variety of language courses including Arabic, Tagalog, Thai.      <u>     </u>

**4**  Educational multimedia can be delivered via CD-ROM or over the Internet.      <u>     </u>

**5**  Flight number 823 from Kuala Lumpur is delayed.      <u>     </u>

**6**  I'd like to speak to the Managing Director, please.      <u>     </u>

Now check your answers in the Answer key.

---

Please turn to Exercises 45 and 46 in Unit 2 for more information on intonation in the context of the IELTS Speaking Test.

## Understanding vocabulary

**READ ME**

To succeed in the Listening Test, naturally it is important to understand the words which the speakers use. This means two things: you need to *know* as many words as possible and you need to be able to guess the meaning of the words that you *don't* know.

### Learning useful words

You can't learn every new word you encounter. You should only try to learn (memorise) words which are useful. There are two types of useful vocabulary for IELTS candidates. They are illustrated in the following table.

**EXAMPLES**

| Useful words | Examples | |
|---|---|---|
| **Versatile words** words which can be used in many different situations and topics | *complex* *aspect* | Football/physics/traffic/conservation/ abortion/politics is a *complex* subject which has many different *aspects*. |
| | *excessive* | *Excessive* eating/drinking/work/ shopping is not good. |
| | *plunge* | The dollar/temperature/price/percentage/ aircraft *plunged*. |
| **Specific words** words which are used in specific situations and topics that you are targeting | | In this case you are targeting the IELTS test. Some of the possible situations and topics are those which are associated with: |
| | *due date* | university |
| | *real estate* | accommodation |
| | *route* | transport |
| | *seat belt* | travel |
| | *deposit* | social services, such as banking |
| | *leisure* | recreation. |

## Exercise 14: Learning useful words

Listen to the tape. Identify the words in the following paragraph which are new for you. Then decide which of these words you would consider learning.

Now he works as a tutor in molecular science at one of the local colleges. Apparently he earns around 50 per cent more than he used to. The workload is relatively heavy, but he has a reasonable amount of annual vacation. By and large, he's satisfied with his new position.

**READ ME**    Learning new words is a large, ongoing task. It requires steady attention, like practising a sport or another skill. For each new word that you want to learn, first check that you understand its:

- meaning(s)
- class ('part of speech', for example, it is an 'adjective')
- usage (you know how to use it in a sentence)
- level of formality (is it slang or formal?)
- correct pronunciation (including stress)

Then you have to memorise the new word. Here are some techniques that you can try:

- Say new words aloud many times.
- Write new words many times.
- Write new words down on pieces of paper and put them in places where you will see them often.
- Turn an exercise book into your personal 'dictionary', dividing it into categories (eg university, feelings, food, action verbs) rather than alphabetically, and slowly adding words.
- Create a simple example to help you remember a new word (eg if you want to remember the word 'workload' you could create a sentence like *Doctors usually have heavy workloads*).

It is useful to learn synonyms, that is words which have the same (or similar) meanings. Sometimes in the IELTS Listening Test you need to match what you hear on the tape with what you see on the question paper. This match may involve synonyms. You can use a thesaurus and a dictionary to help you learn synonyms. An English-English dictionary is useful for learning synonyms.

## Exercise 15: Learning synonyms

Provide at least three synonyms for each of the following words. Where possible find out the differences between the synonyms. One has been done for you as an example.

| 1 | friend | *pal* (colloquial); *mate* (colloquial); *colleague* (at work) |
|---|--------|----------------------------------------------------------------|
| 2 | man | |
| 3 | good | |
| 4 | bad | |
| 5 | big | |
| 6 | to reduce | |

Now check your answers in the Answer key.

## Guessing

READ ME

Even if you learn a lot of words, you will still encounter some that you do not know. Even in your native language you do not always know the meaning of every word that you hear and you have to guess. This skill of guessing is even more necessary when you are listening to a foreign language (and when you are doing the IELTS Listening Test).

We guess the meaning of unfamiliar words by looking at the context of the word (the surrounding words/ideas) and using logic and our knowledge of the world to figure out what the word might mean. For example: *I bought an old radio made out of bakelite.* Less skillful listeners hear the word *bakelite* and say to themselves 'I don't know what that word means', panic, and stop listening. Skillful listeners hear the word, quickly judge the context, say to themselves 'I guess it means some kind of material', and calmly keep listening.

 17

## Exercise 16: Guessing

Below are some words that may be new for you. Listen to the tape and guess the meaning of each word based on what you hear. Then check the dictionary to see if your guesses were (approximately) correct. One has been done for you as an example.

1 bakelite      *some kind of material, maybe a hard material like metal or plastic*

2 pediatrician

3 jingles

4 embezzlement

5 allamanda

6 hardy

## UNDERSTANDING WHAT SPEAKERS ARE DOING

People always have a reason for speaking, that is, they are trying to *do* things when they speak. For example, they may want to explain, thank, apologise, invite, complain, persuade, etc. If you can determine what speakers are *doing*, it will be easier to understand what they are *saying*.

You are able to figure out what people are doing when they speak because you:

- can understand what they are saying

- are familiar with some of the standard ways of doing these things (eg you know that when people make a request they often use words like *would you mind* or *could you* or *please*, and the way they speak sounds like a question)

- can see the big picture (the context) (eg you can see that if the speakers are at an airline check-in desk they are probably doing things like requesting, asking for information, explaining, and/or thanking).

### What speakers do in the IELTS Listening Test

In the IELTS Listening Test speakers have conversations and present monologues.

| CONVERSATIONS (2 or more people talking to each other) | | MONOLOGUES (1 person speaking) | |
|---|---|---|---|
| **Section 1** | **Section 3** | **Section 2** | **Section 4** |
| A conversation between two people. | A conversation between three or four people. | A speaker making an announcement or presenting some information to an audience. | A speaker presenting a talk to an audience. |
| Speakers do things like greeting, giving and asking for information about things and about themselves, requesting, explaining, giving and asking for opinions, or talking about events, plans, and preferences. | | A single speaker does things like giving information, explaining, advising, warning, arguing, describing, comparing, classifying, or describing processess. | |

### Figuring out what the speaker is doing

Normally you use the following three types of information together to work out what the speaker is doing:

1  Your knowledge of vocabulary: What are the key words the speakers are using?

2  Your judgment about the speakers' attitudes: How do the speakers sound (angry, happy, confused, etc)?

3  The context (the situation): Who are the speakers and where are they?

**18**

**EXAMPLE**

Listen to the woman speaking on the tape. Three questions will help you decide what she is *doing*:

1 How does she sound?
*She sounds angry/upset.*

2 What is the context (situation)?
*She is in a supermarket (speaking to the manager).*

3 What are some of the key words she uses?
*really unhappy, disgusting.*

When you consider these three answers together, you can see that she is COMPLAINING.

 **19**

---

### Exercise 17: Understanding what speakers are doing

Listen to the five situations. In each situation, decide what the woman (the first speaker) is doing. The first one has been done for you as an example. If necessary, you can listen to each situation twice before deciding.

**1** How does she sound?     happy, warm, positive

What is the context (situation)? a university (because of 'pass', 'distinction', 'student union')

What are some of the key words she uses? good news, wonderful, well done, happy for you

What is she doing?     She is CONGRATULATING (the other person).

**2** How does she sound? _____

What is the context (situation)? _____

What are some of the key words she uses? _____

What is she doing? _____

**3** How does she sound? _____

What is the context (situation)? _____

What are some of the key words she uses? _____

What is she doing? _____

**4** How does she sound? _____

What is the context (situation)? _____

What are some of the key words she uses? _____

What is she doing? _____

**5** How does she sound? _____

What is the context (situation)? _____

What are some of the key words she uses? _____

What is she doing? _____

## Anticipating

READ ME

When people speak (whether in a conversation or a monologue), they use words which help the listener to work out where the conversation or monologue is going next (words such as *however*, *although*, *because*, *that*, *but*, and *on the other hand*). For example:

> The food at that restaurant was fantastic <u>but</u> the service …

Because you know that *but* introduces a contrast, you can anticipate that the next statement will be negative (something like: *but the service was terrible*).

We can call these words 'link words' because they link two different pieces of information (for example, 'food fantastic'/'service terrible') or 'signpost words' because they show you what direction the speaker is going to take. Good listeners catch these link/signpost words and use them to anticipate what the speaker is going to do next (explain, compare, etc). This helps them follow conversations and monologues more successfully.

---

### Exercise 18: Recognising signpost words

In the left-hand column there are a number of incomplete statements, each containing a common signpost word (these are in **bold**). What do these signpost words tell you about what is coming next? Select your answers from the options in the box and write the appropriate letter beside the statement. One has been done for you as an example.

| | | | |
|---|---|---|---|
| **A** | describe a cause | **E** | express a contrast |
| **B** | give an example/illustration | **F** | make a comparison |
| **C** | describe a condition and a consequence* | **G** | provide further information |
| **D** | introduce a classification* | | |

(* Refer to pages 29 to 35 if you are unsure of their meaning.)

1  He was hoping that the weather would be fine **but** …     E

2  Three students will have to repeat the assignment, **namely** Mark, …     _____

3  He is allowed to take the test again **provided that** …     _____

4  There are so many ways to improve your fitness, **for instance** …     _____

5  Women tend to express their feelings more openly **while** men …     _____

6  The outdoor concert had to be cancelled **due to** …     _____

7  People living in rural areas tend to be **more** conservative **than** …     _____

8  To everyone's surprise he was given a promotion at work **despite** …     _____

9  There are many different varieties of snakes.
   Broadly, they **can be divided into** …     _____

10  **Although** she was very nervous in the interview, she …     _____

11  You can get calcium in many foods **such as** …     _____

12  This photocopier is **not as** clear **as** …     _____

13  He thought the boss would change his mind. **However**, …     _____

14  **If** she passes the test, she will …     _____

---

**20**

### Exercise 19: Anticipating

In situations 1 to 7 below, decide what you think the speaker is going to do next. The first two have been done as examples. Then listen to the tape and see if you have anticipated correctly.

| You hear the speaker say this: | What do you think the speaker is going to do next? |
|---|---|
| **1** I withdrew my application because | give a reason |
| **2** She was hoping to get the job, but | describe what happened (for example, she was not selected) |
| **3** There are three main types of computer. | |
| **4** It's a bit cool. Would you mind if | |
| **5** Using solar power has many advantages. | |
| **6** This is a Channel 4 news update. There has been a three-car accident on the South Freeway. | |
| **7** Good afternoon, ladies and gentlemen. Thank you for that warm welcome. My topic today is | |

 **21**

### Exercise 20: Anticipating

You are going to listen to a short presentation about gardens. Throughout the presentation there are brief pauses. Each time you hear a pause, anticipate:

- what the speaker is going to do next
  (for example, give a reason, express a contrast, etc);

  and/or

- what words the speaker might say next.

As the speaker continues, check whether you have anticipated correctly.

When people speak, they do many things, such as greeting, thanking, explaining, requesting, describing their plans, and so on. In the following exercise you will listen to some of the things people do when they have conversations.

**22**

### Exercise 21: Listening to what speakers are doing

Listen to the conversations and tick the table below when you hear the speakers doing these things. Some of them may occur more than once. The first one has been done for you as an example.

| What the speakers are doing | Conversations | | | | | |
|---|---|---|---|---|---|---|
| | 1 | 2 | 3 | 4 | 5 | 6 |
| asking for information | ✓ | | | | | |
| giving information | ✓ | | | | | |
| thanking | ✓ | | | | | |
| asking an opinion | | | | | | |
| expressing an opinion | | | | | | |
| agreeing | | | | | | |
| offering/inviting | ✓ | | | | | |
| expressing surprise | | | | | | |
| reassuring someone | | | | | | |

When you finish, check your answers in the Answer key. Then look at the Transcript (with a study partner, if possible) and circle the words the speakers use to do these things.

### Exercise 22: Listening to what speakers are doing

Listen to the tape of people talking on the bus and decide what the speakers are doing. Select from the possible answers in the box. One has been done for you as an example.

| | | | |
|---|---|---|---|
| asking for information | requesting | inviting | asking for advice |
| reassuring | arguing | declining | greeting |
| describing | giving advice | insisting | |

1  *greeting* _____

2  _____

3  _____

4  _____

5  _____

6  _____

7  _____

8  _____

9  _____

10 _____

## Other things that speakers do

**READ ME**  There are many things that speakers do in conversations and monologues. Naturally it is not possible to predict which ones will occur in the IELTS Listening Test. The best way to prepare for the test is to have extensive practice in listening to a very wide range of conversations and monologues (for suggestions about how to do this see Unit 1: 5 'Developing your study program'). You should also participate in conversations yourself (See 'Speaking accurately and appropriately' in Unit 2: 5 of this book).

A number of conversations and monologues are also presented below for you to listen to and practise listening for specific information.

## Numbers, times, dates and letters

One very common thing that people do in conversations and monologues is to give information. This information may include times, dates, numbers, and letters. The IELTS Listening Test, especially in Section 1, may check your ability to understand times, dates, numbers, and letters as spoken by native speakers. Listen to the following examples.

**EXAMPLE** 24

| CATEGORY | EXAMPLES |
|----------|----------|
| times | a quarter past four, ten to nine, half past twelve |
| dates | the fifth of March, the twenty-first of November, the thirteenth of February |
| numbers | three point five, seventeen, seventy, fifth, three quarters, eight and a half million |
| letters | UN, USA, S-t-e-v-e-n, IBM, c-a-t-e-g-o-r-y, M-a-r-i-a, c-l-i-c-k |

 25

### Exercise 23: Listening for numbers, times, dates, and letters

Questions 1 to 15

Write NO MORE THAN THREE WORDS OR NUMBERS for each answer.

**1** What is the caller's membership number? _____

**2** What is the surname currently written on her library card? _____

**3** What is the correct spelling of her family name? _____

**4** What is her first name?_____

**5** What is her full address? _____ Clapham_____

**6** When was her book due to be returned? _____

**7** What is the new due date for returning her book?_____

**8** What is her mother's hobby? _____

**9** Who wrote the book she is looking for? _____

**10** When does she think the book was published?_____

**11** When is she going to collect the book? _____

**12** What time does the library open during the week? _____

**13** What time does the library close during the week? _____

**14** What time does the library close on a Sunday?_____

**15** What is the librarian's name? _____

### Procedures and processes

**READ ME** Speakers sometimes describe procedures (what you should do) and processes (how things are done). For example:

> Fill in this form, attach a photo, and submit it to the visa section. Your application will then be considered and you will notified by mail.

### Typical features of processes and procedures

- descriptions of sequence (*first*; *then*; *after that*; *finally*)

- instructions (imperatives such as '*lift* the lid'; '*switch on* the power'; '*click on* start' or words such as 'the first thing you *should* do is ...', 'then you *need* to wait ...')

- descriptions of steps in the process (passive verb forms such as 'the water *is heated*'; 'the impurities *are removed*'; 'the water *is bottled*').

26

---

### Exercise 24: Listening to processes

Listen to the tape and complete questions 1 to 5 in the table below.

Write NO MORE THAN THREE WORDS for each answer.

**Flour milling**

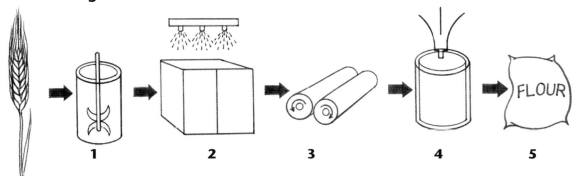

| Stage | Cleaning | (1) | (2) | Bleaching | (5) |
|---|---|---|---|---|---|
| Equipment | bins | sprinklers | (3) | vats | sacks |
| Result | removes dirt/debris | makes the kernels soft | splits the kernels | makes the flour (4) | packs the flour |

---

### Descriptions of objects

**READ ME**    Speakers sometimes describe objects. For example:

> This is a gas heater. Here are the controls: the on-off button is here on the left, and this is the temperature control.

### Typical features of descriptions of objects

- descriptions of location (*in*; *behind*; *in front of*; *below*; *to the left of*)

- descriptions of components (*consist of*; *comprise*; *made of*)

- descriptions of operation (it *moves*; *slides*; *grinds*; *chops*; *removes*; *filters*; *measures*).

---

**Exercise 25: Listening to a description of an object**

Listen to the tape and label the diagram of the barometer.

Write NO MORE THAN THREE WORDS for each answer.

**(1)** _____ Barometer means non- _____ **(2)**

(6) _____

(5) _____

(4) _____

Needle

Vacuum chamber

(3) _____

---

## Descriptions of cause/effect

**READ ME**    Speakers sometimes explain cause and effect. For example:

> Children nowadays are more violent because of the television they watch and the computer games they play.

Here the 'cause' is television and computer games and the 'effect' (or result) is violence among children.

### Typical features of cause/effect statements

- words which link the cause and effect such as *because*; *be due to*; *can be attributed to*; *result from*; *cause*; *lead to*.

---

**Exercise 26: Listening to cause and effect**

Listen to the tape. As you listen, decide if each of the items in the list below is a cause (**C**) or an effect (**E**). One has been done for you as an example.

**Example**    his flight was delayed          *C*  _____

**1**  driver fatigue                              _____

**2**  5% fall in the New York stock exchange      _____

**3**  endless delays                              _____

**4**  she didn't pass the medical                 _____

**5**  massive increase in flooding                _____

---

### Comparisons

Speakers often compare things. For example:

Long-distance telephone calls at the weekend are usually quite a bit cheaper than calls during the week.

### Typical features of comparisons

- words that link the things being compared, such as *whereas; on the other hand; but; although; while; than; not as … as*

- words that describe the comparison, such as *same; similar; different; older; oldest; (much) more* beautiful; *most* beautiful; *less; the least.*

 **29**

---

**Exercise 27: Listening to comparisons**

Listen to the tape and complete the table below.

|  | Trinidad | Tobago |
|---|---|---|
| **Area** | 4828 km$^2$ | 300 km$^2$ |
| **Shape** | (1) _____ | (2) _____ |
| **Elevation** | (3) _____ m. | (4) _____ m. |
| **Percentage of population** | (5) _____ % | (6) _____ % |
| **Year colonised by Britain** | (7) _____ | (8) _____ |

When you finish, check your answers in the Answer key. Then read the Transcript and identify the speaker's link words (eg *whereas*) and comparison words (eg *bigger*).

---

### Classifications

Speakers sometimes classify. For example:

There are three kinds of bus ticket available: daily, weekly, or monthly.

### Typical features of classifications

- words such as *there are; kinds; types; sorts; ways; can be divided into.*

**Exercise 28: Listening to classifications**

Listen to the tape and complete the classification diagrams below. The first one has been done for you as an example.

**1**

**AIRFARES**

| **FIRST CLASS** | **BUSINESS CLASS** | **ECONOMY CLASS** |
|---|---|---|
| **$ 1,350** | $ 1,030 | $ 650 |

**2**

TESTS

Academic Test

English

Computer Literacy

Mathematics

(1) _____ Test

(2) _____

(3) _____

… continued over

... continued

**3**

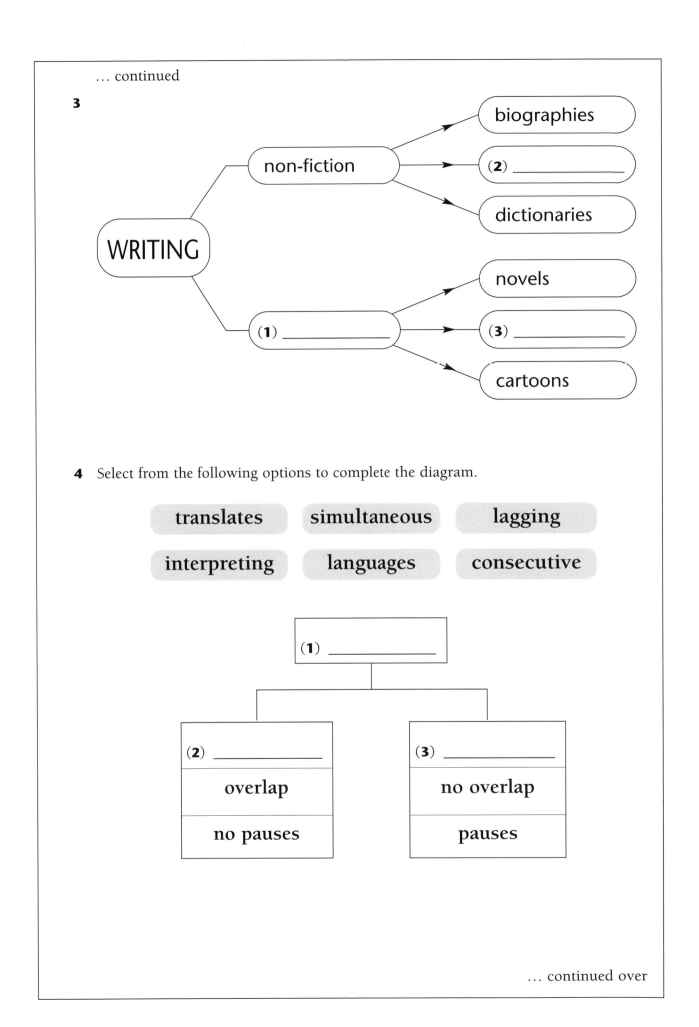

**4** Select from the following options to complete the diagram.

translates    simultaneous    lagging

interpreting    languages    consecutive

(1) _____

(2) _____ | (3) _____
overlap | no overlap
no pauses | pauses

... continued over

... continued

**5**

| Name of bird | (1) _____ | |
|---|---|---|
| (2) _____ | Western | Eastern |
| (3) _____ | • darker colour | • lighter colour |
| | • develops white collar around neck when breeding | • does not change colour when breeding |

 **31**

## Exercise 29: Listening to classifications

Listen to the tape and produce your own classification diagram for each of the three speakers. Then check the Answer key. Note: you will not be asked to produce your own diagrams in the IELTS Listening Test, but it is good practice for developing your listening skills.

## Arguments

**READ ME**     Speakers sometimes 'argue' (present and support their opinions).

### Typical features of arguments

- the speaker presents a position/opinion/viewpoint;
  for example, 'I *think/believe* we *should/ought* to adopt this method'

- to support this, the speaker may present:

  – evidence; for example, 'in the research study, injuries fell by 20%'

  – comparisons; for example, 'this method is safer'

  – reasons; for example, 'because it will reduce accident'

  – examples; for example, 'for instance' in factories.

 **32**

## Exercise 30: Listening to arguments

Listen to the speaker and answer the questions.

Questions 1 and 2

**T** = **T**om
**M** = **M**rs Blake
**D** = **D**iane
**J** = **J**ulie

**1**  Who is in favour of continuous assessment?          _____

**2**  Who is in favour of formal examinations?          _____

When you finish, check your answers in the Answer key. Then look at the Transcript and underline the reasons which people give to support their opinions.

**33**

---

### Exercise 31: Listening to arguments

Listen to speakers 1 to 5. As you listen, decide whether the speaker agrees or disagrees with the statements listed below.

**1**   We should use more solar power.

**2**   Anti-drug television commercials can be very effective.

**3**   Distance study has many advantages.

**4**   Marine pollution is not as serious as we first thought.

**5**   Boxing should be banned.

When you finish, check your answers in the Answer key. Then look at the Transcript (with a study partner, if possible) and underline some of the evidence, comparisons, reasons and examples which support the five conclusions.

---

In the next section of this unit (Unit 1: 5) there are some suggestions for further independent practice of all of these different listening skills.

# 5 Developing your study program

To prepare for the IELTS Listening Test you need to devise a study program that will help you develop your listening strategies and skills.

- First decide what your needs are.

- Then choose some materials to practise your listening.

- Then practise the strategies and skills required by the Listening Test.

## DECIDING YOUR NEEDS

**READ ME**

Think about what you need. For example, do you need to focus on understanding pronunciation or on listening for specific information or checking your understanding of what is in the listening test? Tick those items that you need to work on in your study program.

---

### Listening checklist ( ✓ )

**Which aspects of the IELTS Listening Test do you need to check?**

| | |
|---|---|
| the length of the test | ( ) |
| the number of sections | ( ) |
| the number of questions | ( ) |
| the types of questions | ( ) |
| how instructions are given | ( ) |
| transferring answers to the Answer Sheet | ( ) |

**Which listening strategies do you need to improve?**

| | |
|---|---|
| listening for specific information | ( ) |
| focusing on more than one question at the same time | ( ) |
| matching the meaning | ( ) |

**Which listening skills do you need to improve?**

| | |
|---|---|
| understanding pronunciation | ( ) |
| guessing the meaning | ( ) |
| matching the meaning | ( ) |
| learning new vocabulary | ( ) |
| anticipating | ( ) |
| listening for detailed information | ( ) |
| listening for processes | ( ) |
| listening for comparisons | ( ) |
| listening for classifications | ( ) |
| listening for arguments | ( ) |

---

## FINDING APPROPRIATE MATERIALS TO PRACTISE LISTENING

Your first listening resource is the tape accompanying this book. Do all the exercises on the tape as you read through the unit. Later in your study program, you can use the exercises *again*, but this time for different purposes. For example, Exercise 2 gives practice in 'listening for specific information', but later in your study program you can listen to that same exercise to practise a different skill; for example, 'focusing on more than one question' or 'guessing', depending on what you see as your priority needs. Use the tape as your personal resource.

You can also create your own practice materials by interviewing people and recording the interviews. Your interviews should have a clear and useful purpose; for example, find people who have already successfully completed the IELTS and ask them what they did to prepare for the Listening Test.

### English-language radio programs

Try finding national and international English-language radio stations.

If you are in an English-speaking country, you will have ready access to a wide variety of English language radio stations. Tune in to stations that feature interviews or 'talk-back' (where listeners telephone the station to give their views on current issues).

If you are in a non-English speaking country, try to tune in to stations such as the BBC World Service, the Voice of America, the Canadian Broadcasting Corporation, or Radio Australia.

### Television

Watch English language television as much as possible. Look for material which features conversations (eg soap operas, talk shows, etc) and announcements/presentations (eg news/current affairs programs, documentaries). Videotape these programs to watch again later for closer analysis of language.

### The Internet

Do a search for relevant websites on the Internet. Use a reliable search engine like Google (www.google.com) or Mamma (www.mamma.com) to discover IELTS practice resources in cyberspace. A useful starting point for IELTS resources would be the official IELTS site at www.ielts.org. The Web is also a useful resource for material to back up listening material which is broadcast on radio and TV around the world. Broadcasting organisations such as the ABC (www.abc.net.au) have transcripts of their radio and television programs and also allow users to listen to selected material via their websites. Other sites that have listening materials for users include BBC Online (www.bbc.co.uk) and CNN (www.cnn.com). New websites are being created all the time (and existing websites change), so do keep searching.

### Textbooks and audio-visual resources

These are the best source of material for structured listening practice. Look for materials which contain conversations, announcements and short presentations/lectures at an upper-intermediate or advanced level. Listening preparation materials for other exams such as TOEFL and Cambridge Certificate in Advanced English can also be useful for IELTS if used selectively.

For all the materials you gather, try to find listenings which present both male and female speakers using a range of accents, and which involve both individual and multiple speakers. It is also useful to have transcripts of your listening materials. The first time you listen to the material, you should listen without reading the transcript. Use the transcript for follow-up listening.

Below are some suggested textbooks/resources. All of them have accompanying cassettes.

### Practice for IELTS Listening Test Sections 1, 2 and 3

McEvedy, M P and P Wyatt 1990. *Listen and do*. Perth: Western Australia College of Advanced Education

Numrich, C 1994. *Raise the issues: An integrated approach to critical thinking*. New York: Longman

Numrich, C 1995. *Consider the issues*. New York: Longman

Pidcock, J 1990. *Progressive listening*. Surrey: Nelson

Rixon, S 1987. *Listening: Upper intermediate*. Oxford: Oxford University Press

Robinson, C 1986. *Themes for listening and speaking*. Oxford: Oxford University Press

Scarborough, D 1984. *Reasons for listening*. Cambridge: Cambridge University Press

### Practice for IELTS Listening Test Section 4

James, G 1992. *Interactive listening on campus: Authentic academic mini-lectures*. Boston, Mass: Heinle and Heinle

Kisslinger, E 1994. *Selected topics: High intermediate listening comprehension*. New York: Longman

Mangubhai, F and J Everingham 1991. *Listening: Developing skills in English*. Toowoomba: University of Southern Queensland Press

### PRACTISING THE STRATEGIES AND SKILLS NEEDED FOR THE LISTENING TEST

**READ ME**

You should have two overall aims in listening to the material you gather:

1 Listen to as much material as possible.

2 Have a focus when you are listening; that is, focus on practising the different strategies and skills you have learned about in Unit 1: 3 and Unit 1: 4.

### Exercises for independent study

### Listen for specific information

When using textbooks to practise listening, look at the questions carefully first and decide what specific information you need to listen for in order to answer the questions (review Exercises 1 to 4 as a reminder of this strategy). Practise the strategy when you do any listening exercises, and be sure to apply it when you do the IELTS Practice Test.

You can also make up your own focus questions when you listen to material you have recorded yourself. For example, before you watch the television news, set yourself some simple questions to focus your listening; such as:

What is the first news item about today?

How many stories mention England?

List all of the countries mentioned today.

How many positive/happy stories are there today?

How many news stories today will mention the word 'injured' or 'injury'?

## Focus on more than one question

When doing the IELTS Listening Test, you will need to focus on more than one question at a time so that you do not miss an answer and fall behind. Look at Exercises 5 and 6 as examples. Practise this strategy when you do other exercises (for example, Exercises 7, 23 to 25, 27) and apply it when you do the IELTS Practice Test.

To practise this strategy by yourself, you need to have sets of questions ready before listening. One easy set of questions to remember and use is the 'wh-' set: *who, what, when, what time, where, why* (and maybe *how*). You could choose just a few of these. When you are listening to the radio news, television news, or the practice exercises on the tape, you can be ready to answer three questions. For example: *Who* is this about? *What* happened? *Where* did it happen? In this way, you are focusing on three questions at the same time, as you will need to do in the IELTS. As you become more confident, you can add more of the 'wh-' questions to your set. As you listen, you can make notes to help answer the questions. If you are listening to the radio or television news, you can check your answers during the next news broadcast.

## Match the meaning

When matching what you see in the IELTS question paper with what you hear on the tape, you try to find the same meaning, not just the same words. Look at Exercises 7 and 8 as examples. You can practise matching the meaning when you do multiple-choice questions (for example, Exercise 3a). Look at the answers offered and think of other ways of saying them. Then listen to the tape and match.

If you have access to English newspapers and English television or radio broadcasts, you can do a multimedia match. First read the headlines of, say, three stories on the front page of the newspaper. Think of other ways of expressing the same meaning as the headlines. Think of synonyms that could be used. Then listen to the news on the television or radio to hear what words are used to convey the same meaning. If possible, record the broadcast so that you can compare the different versions more closely. Learn any useful synonyms you find.

## Listen to what people are saying

To catch what people are saying in the IELTS test, you must be able to understand their pronunciation and their vocabulary. To practise listening to people, it is best to use cassettes. In this way you can pause and repeat as much as necessary. You can record from television, radio, classrooms (with permission) and the Internet. You can interview people and record it.

It is also useful to do as much real-life listening as is available to you (for example, at the bus stop, at the airport, or on radio). Listen to the way people pronounce words. Note how people stress words. Listen to their intonation. Focus on some of the points practised in Exercises 9 to 13.

If you have recordings of native speakers, transcribe what you hear and ask an appropriate person to correct your transcription. If there are errors, see how these errors might relate to difficulties you have in listening to native-speaker pronunciation.

A useful exercise for independent study is to listen to a short talk in English – you need to have a transcript of the talk available so you can check it later. Any subject is suitable for the talk as long as it is not too technical. As you play the cassette, listen to how the speaker pronounces words. You may need to listen several times. As a follow-up exercise, you could listen again and count the number of words in particular sentences or transcribe a paragraph. It is likely that you will under-estimate the number of words that you hear. This is because many words are contracted or unstressed in spoken English.

To learn how intonation is used in English, listen to any conversation or short talk/lecture in English and mark the words that are strongly stressed on the transcript. This will show you how speakers use stress to highlight information. Think about why certain words are stressed. Is it to give opposite or contrasting information? Is it to add information?

Practise the skill of guessing. Try to catch new words when listening to a news story on the radio or television (key words are often repeated several times in a story). Then cross-check that story in a newspaper to look for the new words. Then check them in a dictionary and thesaurus.

Take note of any useful new words you find. Keep expanding your vocabulary.

## Listen to what people are doing

You need to be able to follow what people are 'doing' when they speak, whether they are, for example, apologising, describing, comparing or complaining. Look at Exercises 21 to 31 as examples.

For further practice, every time you listen, ask yourself what you are listening to – is it a conversation or a monologue (an announcement, presentation, or lecture)? More specifically, ask yourself what the speaker is doing; for example, comparing, greeting, explaining, apologising, describing a process, and so on. You can also do this in real-life listening. What are the people (in the seat in front of you, for example) doing? Are they chatting about the weather, discussing their plans, teasing each other, or complaining about their homework?

To learn more about the words and grammatical structures which people use to do all these different things ('functions'), look at J Blundell 1982. *Function in English*. Oxford: Oxford University Press.

Another important skill to practise is anticipating, knowing what the speaker is going to say or do *next*. Look at Exercise 19 as an example. To practise this, use the cassette accompanying this book. Stop the cassette at different points and see if you can anticipate what the speaker is going to say or do next. Then continue listening and see how accurately you anticipated.

You can also practise this strategy when you are watching television. For example, you could videotape English language 'soap operas' from the TV and then play them back, pausing the video in a dramatic scene and anticipating what your favourite character is going to say next. Start the tape again and check whether your prediction was right. You can also practise this (in your mind) when you are listening to live speakers.

## Exercises for study partners

If possible, choose a partner of the same English language level – maybe someone from your class who wants to do the IELTS test at the same time as you. It would be a good idea if this person spoke a different first language from you, so you can work solely in English.

Having a study partner to practise listening with can be enjoyable and motivating. Another advantage is that you can prepare questions for each other. Here are some exercises you can do with a partner.

### Write short-answer questions

Choose a listening passage with a transcript. Write a series of 'wh-' questions based on information in the passage. Look at Exercise 23 as an example. Give the questions to your partner and allow him/her 30 seconds to read the questions. Then read the passage aloud once, without pausing.

### Make gap-filling exercises

To practise gap-filling exercises, you need to have two copies of a passage. On one copy make gaps by deleting information or content words. Every 10 to 15 words, delete from one to four words (if you delete several words, make sure that they form a 'phrase', that is they are related in meaning). Give this copy to your partner to fill in, while you read out the complete copy.

It is also good practice to use passages which are accompanied by diagrams, flowcharts, or tables. Delete some information on the graphic and give it to your partner to complete while you read the passage aloud (look at Exercise 25 as an example).

### Listen and compare

You and your study partner could watch English language movies on TV or video together. After key scenes, discuss what you have heard. Try to summarise in words how the scene develops the narrative (story) of the film and anticipate what will come next. You could even try to remember the dialogue of a particular scene and act it out with your partner, noting key vocabulary, and copying pronunciation patterns from what you hear.

# 6 IELTS practice test: Listening

This practice Listening Test has been written to simulate the IELTS in its style, format, and length. In taking the test, you should simulate IELTS test conditions. This means that you should do the test by yourself. You should sit at a distance from the cassette recorder, and play the tape only once, without pausing or stopping. When you finish the test, check the Answer key.

 **34**

## IELTS PRACTICE TEST: LISTENING

TIME ALLOWED: 30 minutes

NUMBER OF QUESTIONS: 40

### Instructions

You will hear a number of different recordings and you will have to answer questions on what you hear.

There will be time for you to read the instructions and questions and you will have a chance to check your work.

All the recordings will be played **ONCE** only.

The test is in four sections. Write your answers in the listening section booklet.

**At the end of the test you will be given ten minutes to transfer your answers to an answer sheet.**

Now turn to Section 1 on the next page.

## SECTION 1    QUESTIONS 1 TO 10

### Questions 1 to 6

Which information is correct? Tick (✔) if the information is correct **or** write in the changes.

| | |
|---|---|
| **The apartment is number 34.** | ✔ |
| **The apartment is on the fourth floor.** | third |
| The view from the apartment is terrible. | **(1)** _____ |
| The apartment is close to the university. | **(2)** _____ |
| The apartment is very secure. | **(3)** _____ |
| The apartment is quite large. | **(4)** _____ |
| The furniture is included in the rent. | **(5)** _____ |
| Michael thinks there is too much storage. | **(6)** _____ |

### Questions 7 to 10

Write NO MORE THAN THREE WORDS for each answer.

**7** How many apartments must share the laundry?  _____

**8** What time is the appointment tomorrow?  _____

**9** What is the telephone number of the man who will come to the apartment tomorrow?  _____

**10** What is the name (first name and family name) of the man who will come to the apartment tomorrow?  _____

## SECTION 2    QUESTIONS 11 TO 20

### Questions 11 to 15

Listen to the first part of Alison's briefing and answer questions 11 to 15.

Write NO MORE THAN THREE WORDS for each answer.

**Example:**

This briefing is for                                    *new staff*                    .


Alison's position is (**11**)                                    _____.

This is a high-security building because it has a (**12**)                _____.

The only method of opening the security door is
to use a (**13**)                                    _____.

If staff forget their PIN, they should speak to the (**14**)                _____.

The card should be passed through the machine
smoothly and (**15**)                                    _____.

### Questions 16 to 18

Complete the table showing the **information** which visitors must provide.

Write NO MORE THAN THREE WORDS for each answer.

| VISITORS' REGISTER | | | | | | |
|---|---|---|---|---|---|---|
| Name | Organisation | (**16**) | Staff contact | (**17**) | (**18**) | Time out |

### Questions 19 and 20

Circle the correct letter **A**, **B** or **C**.

**19** What does the security officer issue to visitors?

    **A**  a visitor's card

    **B**  a staff card

    **C**  a visitors' register

**20** Which column must the visitor fill in after the visit?

    **A**  time out

    **B**  procedures

    **C**  staff contact

## SECTION 3    QUESTIONS 21 TO 30

### Questions 21 to 27

Listen to the conversation between three university students and answer the questions below. Circle the correct letter **A**, **B** or **C**.

**21** What year is Mary in?

  **A**  first year

  **B**  fourth year

  **C**  second year

**22** How much does it cost to be a member of the Law Students Association for a year?

  **A**  thirty-five pounds

  **B**  twenty-five pounds

  **C**  ten pounds

**23** How much do Law Association members pay to go to the Law Ball?

  **A**  five pounds

  **B**  twenty-five pounds

  **C**  twenty pounds

**24** Why isn't Jack interested in going to the Law Ball?

  **A**  he can't dance

  **B**  he can't get a discount

  **C**  he feels it's not good value

**25** When are guest seminars conducted?

  **A**  tomorrow

  **B**  the first day of the month

  **C**  once a month

**26** Jack can't go to guest seminars because he …

  **A**  is only a first-year student

  **B**  doesn't have enough time

  **C**  prefers other activities

**27** Martin thinks that 'peer coaching' is when …

  **A**  invited guest speakers give presentations

  **B**  people provide a very useful service

  **C**  students combine study and sport

## Questions 28 to 30

Write NO MORE THAN THREE WORDS for each answer.

The law books are cheaper because they are (**28**) _____.

In the end, (**29**) _____ signs up as a member of the Law Students Association but his friend decides not to, because he doesn't have enough (**30**) _____.

## SECTION 4     QUESTIONS 31 TO 40

### Questions 31 to 36

Write NO MORE THAN THREE WORDS for each answer.

**31** How many people in the audience have experienced culture shock?

_____

**32** This lecture will help students complete their _____ assignment.

**33** When the familiar is removed, people experience _____.

**34** What does the speaker discuss as an example of different values in different countries? _____

**35** The speaker compares values to icebergs because they are both mostly

_____.

**36** People who anticipate culture shock generally experience _____ shock than others.

### Questions 37 and 38

In each question, circle TWO letters.

**37** Which TWO of the following are mentioned as the physical symptoms of culture shock? Circle TWO letters.

   **A**  losing appetite

   **B**  turning pale

   **C**  experiencing headaches

   **D**  losing weight

   **E**  forgetting things

   **F**  experiencing cold

**38** Which TWO of the following things does the speaker do in this lecture? Circle TWO letters.

   **A**  He explains the meaning of the term 'culture shock'.

   **B**  He tells the students how to fix culture shock when it happens.

   **C**  He talks about his own experience with culture shock.

   **D**  He claims that culture shock has no impact on physical and mental health.

   **E**  He asks the students to describe their experience with culture shock.

   **F**  He tells the students how to prepare for next week's lecture.

## Questions 39 and 40

Circle the correct letter **A**, **B** or **C**.

**39** Which of the following graphs shows the pattern being described?

**A**

**B**

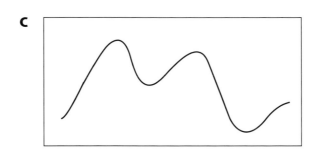

**C**

**40** Which TWO of the following does the speaker recommend when in a new cultural environment? Circle TWO letters.

    **A**  keep smiling

    **B**  take it easy

    **C**  avoid ups and downs

    **D**  learn more

    **E**  have a good time

    **F**  change yourself inside

    **G**  make some adjustments

    **H**  get married

# FOCUSING ON
# IELTS

## LISTENING AND SPEAKING SKILLS

# UNIT 2: Speaking

# 1 What is in the IELTS speaking module?

| | Academic and General Training candidates<br>All candidates do the same speaking test. |
|---|---|
| **Time allowed** | 11 to 14 minutes |
| **Procedure** | The examiner will call you into the examination room from a waiting area. You and the examiner will be alone in the examination room, sitting facing each other with a desk between you.<br><br>The examiner will switch on a cassette-recorder at the beginning of the test. The purpose of this recording is to ensure that the examiner has conducted the test correctly. |
| **Format** | The test consists of three parts, each with a different format. First there is an interview, then a short presentation, and finally a discussion.<br><br>**Part 1: Introduction and interview**<br>(4 to 5 minutes)<br><br>You come into the examination room. You and the examiner exchange greetings and you are invited to sit down. The examiner checks your ID. The examiner tries to get you to 'settle down' (feel relaxed), asking basic questions about your life, your background, and so on.<br><br>**Part 2: Individual long turn**<br>(3 to 4 minutes, including 1 minute to think and prepare)<br><br>The examiner gives you a card with a topic written on it. You have 1 minute to think about this topic and prepare what you are going to say. Then you must speak about the topic for 1 to 2 minutes. After you finish talking, the examiner could ask one or two follow-up questions.<br><br>**Part 3: Two-way discussion**<br>(4 to 5 minutes)<br><br>The examiner engages you in a discussion about topics that have the same general theme as Part 2. |

# 2 Test-taking tips

What should you do when you take the IELTS Speaking Test? Here are some suggestions about how to manage the test as successfully as possible.

## SPEAK AS MUCH AS YOU CAN

**READ ME**

The most important thing you can do in the Speaking Test is to speak as much as possible. You should speak far more than the examiner, who should mainly be listening to what you are saying. If the examiner has to speak more than you do, you won't do well in the test. Especially in Parts 2 and 3 of the test, give as much information as possible to answers and don't ever give one-word answers.

## SPEAK AT A REASONABLE VOLUME AND SPEED

**READ ME**

Speak at an appropriate volume for the examiner to hear you comfortably. Don't whisper and don't shout. Direct your voice at the examiner and not at the tape recorder on the desk. Remember, that if you speak too softly, you may appear lacking in confidence.

Also, be aware that when you are nervous, you will tend to speak more quickly. This may make it more difficult for the examiner to understand you, particularly if you have pronunciation problems.

## MAKE A GOOD IMPRESSION

**READ ME**

The examiner does not evaluate how you look during the test (for example, how you dress, how you sit, how confident you look, and so on), but these things may have an unconscious impact on the examiner's perception of you. Like a job interview, it is important to make a good visual impression:

- Wear neat casual clothes. Dress comfortably, so that you feel as relaxed as possible.

- Manage your posture (the way you walk into the room, the way you hold your body while you sit). Walk into the examination room confidently. During the test, sit in a way that shows you are ready to actively participate, for example, sitting up straight with your body inclined slightly forward. Don't fold your arms across your chest or clasp your hands on your head.

- Manage your non-verbal behaviour. Look directly at the examiner when you first meet and maintain consistent eye contact with him/her throughout the test. Remember that western cultures generally use more sustained eye contact than non-western cultures. Your facial expression should show that you are listening. It is not necessary to smile all the time. Try to reduce any nervous gestures or expressions that you may have, such as giggling (laughing) or fidgeting (moving too much).

## KNOW WHAT TO EXPECT

**READ ME**

Know what to expect in the test. Make sure that you are thoroughly familiar with the structure of the test and make sure that you know what you have to do in each part. You don't have to worry about time management in each part – the examiner will tell you when your time in each part of the test is finished. Like the IELTS Listening Test, the test becomes progressively more difficult. For example, you may find that Part 1 is quite easy, but that in Part 3 you have trouble expressing your ideas in English. Expect this and be prepared.

Remember that the structure of the test is standardised. The examiner must follow standard procedures and questions in conducting each test, so that it is fair for every candidate. This is why the examiner will record your test, so that if necessary, the IELTS authorities can check that the examiner has conducted the test in an appropriate way.

You also should follow standard procedures. Do not ask the examiner:

- personal questions

- your result/score at the end of the test

- to evaluate your performance or to give you feedback at the end of the test.

### DON'T PANIC IF ASKED ABOUT AN UNFAMILIAR TOPIC

**READ ME**

In Part 3 of the test there is a possibility you will be asked to speak about an unfamiliar topic. If you are asked about a subject you know nothing about, you should state your unfamiliarity with this area and then go on to tell the examiner anything you do know about the topic. These may be things directly or indirectly connected to the topic. To speak about related topic areas is better than no response at all. While thinking about your response, you should use a variety of thinking time techniques. For more details on this area, see 'Thinking time techniques/fillers' in Unit 2: 3 and then practise Exercise 10, which follows it.

### DON'T MEMORISE

**READ ME**

It is important to know what to expect in the Speaking Test. This does not mean, however, that you should memorise what you are going to say. The examiner will easily see that you are saying something you have prepared, and will quickly change the topic. It is useful to anticipate the kinds of topics and questions you may encounter in the test (see Unit 2: 3), but this does not mean that you should prepare a fixed 'speech' in advance.

### TRY TO RELAX

**READ ME**

It is natural to be nervous in the Speaking Test. Examiners expect this, so there is no point in your saying something like 'I am very nervous'. To manage your nervousness, try to find relaxation techniques that you can do before the test. For example, while you are waiting for the test to begin, the following techniques can be useful in preparing yourself for the stress of the test: slow, deep breathing; visualisation of relaxing images; and saying positive calming things to yourself. Also, during the test itself, giving yourself a few moments to breathe deeply before replying to a difficult question should improve your performance.

# 3 The speaking strategies you need

The aim of this section is to familiarise you with the structure of the IELTS Speaking Test, to introduce a range of topics that may occur in your interview and to provide help in answering questions about these topics. It will also suggest strategies to consider if you come across unfamiliar topics in the test.

The IELTS examiner is expecting you to speak both fluently and accurately during your interview – mostly about topics you feel comfortable talking about. However, particularly in Part 3, the last section of the Speaking Test, you may also be expected to discuss topics that are more complex.

## PART 1: ANSWERING QUESTIONS ABOUT FAMILIAR/KNOWN TOPICS (4 TO 5 MINUTES)

**READ ME**

In this part of the IELTS Speaking Test you will be asked to identify yourself and to discuss familiar topics related to your personal background.

The first stage of Part 1 is concerned with recording administrative detail. After greeting the candidate and bringing him/her into the room, the examiner will start the tape recorder and record some basic information about the candidate. At this stage, candidates will also be asked for proof of identity. The examiner will also ask here about your preferred 'friendly' name by saying something like 'What should I call you?' Again, keep the answer (and the name) simple.

You will be asked to talk about two or three topics in Part 1, so you need to keep your answers relevant to the topic you have been asked about. In this section you could be using language to *describe, express preferences, give opinions and reasons, explain, suggest, compare and contrast.*

In the first section of Part 1, you could be asked to discuss at least <u>one</u> of the following topics. Please note that this is <u>not</u> a complete list of topics that could occur in this part of the IELTS Speaking Test.

---

### Part 1: Possible topics

#### Your home

*Your family home and surroundings:* appearance, location, size, etc

*Your home town:* physical appearance, notable features, population/size, historical background etc

#### Your job studies

*Job:* Main responsibilities of job, things you like/dislike about it, how long you have been doing it etc

*Studies:* Subjects studied, why you're studying, things you like/dislike about your course, how long you will study, what qualification you will gain etc

---

You should be ready to discuss all aspects of your home, home town, job or studies in this part of the interview.

**EXAMPLE**     Question:     Describe the street where you live [in your home town].

Response:     Well, it's a long street with many tall apartment blocks. The street is wide and usually busy with cars, bikes and other traffic. There isn't much open space and only a few trees.

---

### Exercise 1: Asking and answering questions about your home/job/studies

Use information from the box 'Part 1: Possible topics' to make questions on the topics of home and job/studies. Ask a partner your questions and note the responses. The first one has been done for you as an example.

| Questions about home/job/studies | Responses |
| --- | --- |
| How long have you lived in your home-town? | My family moved there from a small village in the country when I was four. |
|  |  |
|  |  |
|  |  |
|  |  |
|  |  |

When you have finished, check the Answer key for other possible questions and responses about these topics.

---

**READ ME**     After speaking about your home or job/studies, you could be asked to talk about at least <u>one</u> and possibly <u>two</u> general topics that are related to you and/or your personal background. These could include the following:

---

**Part 1: Possible general topics**

1  your family

2  your daily routine

3  your leisure/free time activities

4  your accommodation (where you live)

5  learning English/other languages

6  food and drink

7  your country and culture

---

Again, please note that this is <u>not</u> a complete list of topics that could occur in this section of the IELTS Speaking Test.

## Exercise 2: Predicting and answering questions

Study the subject areas in the list of general topics in the box above. Expand on each subject area by making at least two possible questions and two possible responses for each. Then ask a partner your questions. The first one has been done for you as an example.

| General topic area | Possible questions | Possible responses |
|---|---|---|
| **1** Your family | Do you have a large family? | Yes, I come from a big family. |
| | | No, my family is quite small. |
| | How many brothers and sisters do you have? | I have one brother and one sister. I'm the middle child. |
| | | I am the only child in my family. |
| | Do you still live with your family? | No, I moved out to live by myself last year. |
| **2** Your daily routine | What do you do on Sundays? | I usually … |
| **3** Leisure/free time activities | | I really enjoy _____ ing … |
| **4** Accommodation | | |
| **5** Learning languages | | |
| **6** Food and drink | | |
| **7** Visiting your country/Visitors to your country | | |

**1**

## Exercise 3: Listening to Part 1

Listen to Part 1 of a sample interview. Note in the table below the general subject areas of the questions. Then listen again and note the exact questions the examiner asked. On your final listening, concentrate on the answers given by the candidate and decide whether the answers were clear and related to the question or not. The first question/answer has been done for you as an example.

| General subject area | Exact question asked by examiner | Answer clear and related to question? |
|---|---|---|
| **1** Job/Study | Are you currently studying or do you work? | Yes |
| **2** Study | And why … | |
| **3** | | |
| **4** | | |
| **5** | | |
| **6** | | |
| **7** | | |
| **8** | | |
| **9** | | |
| **10** | | |
| **11** | | |

## PART 2: GIVING A SHORT PRESENTATION (3 TO 4 MINUTES)

**READ ME**  In Part 2 of the IELTS Speaking Test, you are given a topic and then have one minute to prepare a short talk – sometimes called a 'long turn'. You are asked to speak on this topic for between one and two minutes. In this section of the interview, you are encouraged to extend your discourse; that is, to develop one idea thoroughly by using more varied sentence structures and linking words.

In this section you could be using language to *describe, explain, give or justify your opinion, tell a story, summarise* and *suggest*. The topics that you are asked to talk about in Part 2 should be familiar to you.

A particular focus of this section is organising your ideas into a cohesive presentation within the time limit and making your listener understand. You should use a mixture of formal and informal language in your talk, but overall, the register/style of your presentation should be more formal than informal.

## What to do before you speak

You have one minute to prepare what you are going to say. It is important to use all this time and to use it effectively. The first thing to do is to make sure you have understood what you need to talk about. If you are not entirely clear about the topic you have been given, then check your understanding with the examiner.

After you have read and understood the topic, you should think about possible ideas and make some written notes about what you are going to say. The examiner will encourage this by giving you some paper and a pencil to note down ideas. To ensure your talk is organised and follows a clear structure, these notes should relate to the points or 'prompts' listed on the topic card. When your preparation time is finished, the examiner will tell you that you should start speaking. You will be allowed to keep the topic card during your 1 to 2 minute talk.

The following is an example of a topic card from Part 2 of the IELTS Speaking Test.

**EXAMPLE**    Repeat information

---

Describe a personal possession that is valuable to you.

You should say:

What it is

How long you have owned it

How you use it

And explain why it is so significant for you.

---

**READ ME**    In the example above, the central idea involves something you possess or own. You cannot choose to talk about a person like your mother or a friend, it needs to be something you have in your possession. You will notice that the central topic has already been broken down for you into a series of suggested prompts. You can use these points or use your own ideas (or a combination of both) in answering this question.

**EXAMPLE**    Sample notes on topic

---

Describe a personal possession that is valuable to you.

| | |
|---|---|
| What it is | *My gold wedding ring* |
| How long you have owned it | *Since marriage fourteen years ago* |
| How you use it | *Ring finger on my left hand* |
| And explain why it is so significant for you | *Symbolises continuing love and respect for each other.* |

---

## Exercise 4: Practising Part 2

Consider the topic: Describe a personal possession that is valuable to you. In one minute, write some notes about how you would answer this question.

Describe a personal possession that is valuable to you. You should say:

| | |
|---|---|
| What it is | |
| How long you have owned it | |
| How you use it | |
| And explain why it is so significant for you | |
| Other ideas | |

When you have finished, deliver this Part 2 presentation to a partner. Make sure your talk is no longer than two minutes.

**READ ME**  Good ideas and suitable vocabulary are only one part of a successful performance in Part 2. Another focus of the Speaking Test is the ability to extend your answers into complex sentences. There are many linking words in English that are used to expand ideas into complex sentences. These can be common coordinators such as *and* or *but*, subordinators such as *although* or *because*, or conjunctive adverbs such as *however* or *therefore*. An important point to remember is that you should only use connecting words that sound 'natural' when you are using them. For example, you should generally avoid conjunctive adverbs like *moreover* and *thus*, which are primarily used in written English.

 2

## Exercise 5: Extending your answer in Part 2

Now listen to a sample Part 2 presentation on a valuable object. Circle any of the linking words below that you hear.

    and    but    for    nor    or    so    yet

    however    until    which    because    nevertheless    instead

Now check your answers in the Answer key.

## Exercise 6: Further practice for Part 2

Choose one of the topics below. Give yourself one minute to prepare your talk. Make notes about what you are going to speak about. The first topic has been done for you as an example. Then give a two-minute presentation to your partner.

### Topics

**1** A city you would like to visit

Say what city it is

*Rome*

Why you would like to go there

*Architecture*

How long you would stay

*At least a month*

Explain why it is such a special city for you

*Most historic and romantic city in Europe*

**2** A book/movie that I have recently enjoyed

What book/movie it was

_____

Why it was so good

_____

How it differed to other books/movies of the same type

_____

Explain why it was such a special experience for you

_____

**3** A leader who has greatly influenced me

Who he/she is/was

_____

What he/she did that was so significant

_____

What other people think about this person

_____

How he/she personally influenced my life

_____

… continued over

... continued

**4** An unforgettable event in my life

What the event was

_____

Why it was so significant

_____

Who else it was unforgettable for

_____

How it changed your life

_____

Turn to the Answer key for a model answer to the first topic.

## PART 3: PARTICIPATING IN A MORE ABSTRACT DISCUSSION (4 TO 5 MINUTES)

**READ ME**   The final part of the Speaking Test is a two-way discussion. The subject is related to the topic you have spoken about in Part 2. The focus of this section is on developing/expanding an idea into a free-flowing discussion. For example, if the topic of the presentation in Part 2 was about schools or schooling, the topic under discussion in Part 3 could be one of the following:

1   differences between national education systems

2   recent developments in education or educational technology and how they have influenced teaching

3   different styles/methods of teaching and learning between different cultures.

In this section you could be using language to *describe, speculate, evaluate, suggest, identify, assess, explain, consider, predict, exemplify (give examples)* and *compare and contrast.*

Because of the complexity of this section, you may also be using language to *clarify meaning* and *repair communication breakdowns if they occur* (including paraphrasing).

## Exercise 7: Recognising what you are being asked to do

Look at the following list of language functions that you may be required to use in Part 3 of the Speaking Test. Check to make sure you know what they mean. Listed below them are a number of functions of Part 3-type questions. Match a question to a function and write the appropriate letter in the space provided. Use each function once only. The first one has been done for you as an example.

### Functions

| | | | |
|---|---|---|---|
| **A** | Explain | **E** | Identify |
| **B** | Evaluate | **F** | Describe |
| **C** | Contrast | **G** | Suggest |
| **D** | Speculate | **H** | Predict |

### Questions

**1** What will be some major technological trends in the next fifty years?  ___H___

**2** What are some differences in the use of technology between developed and developing countries?  _____

**3** How can we make the best use of technology in education?  _____

**4** Account for the recent explosive growth in online education.  _____

**5** Are the effects of technological change in the field of education always positive?  _____

**6** In your opinion, which school subjects could be taught more effectively by computers?  _____

**7** Will technology ever reach a stage where it is considered perfect, or will it always be changing and evolving?  _____

**8** What makes a good teacher?  _____

When you have finished, check your answers in the Answer key.

**READ ME**    Part 1 and Part 3 of the IELTS Speaking Test are similar in some ways. However, the main difference is that in Part 1 you are simply required to answer the question, while in Part 3 you are expected to give an answer that extends and expands the topic. In particular, the examiner is looking for an answer that uses complex sentences and a wide range of grammatical structures. A more advanced standard of vocabulary use is also desirable in Part 3.

**EXAMPLE**    Question:    Where do you think technology will take us in the next twenty years?

Response:    Well, I think that technology will take us in many new directions, but I think one of the most dynamic areas will be in the area of teaching and learning. For example, in many countries, online courses will replace some classroom-based courses, and students will interact with their teachers in a totally different way.

---

### Exercise 8: Extending your answers in Part 3

Study the questions below. First think of some ideas and then deliver answers to your partner in a cohesive and extended way. The first one has been done for you as an example.

**1** How has technology changed methods of food production in your country in the last fifty years?

#### IDEAS

Before heavy labour for men and women, agricultural machinery not available, limited range of crops planted, all crops sold locally

Now – reduced labour, agricultural machinery available and used on most farms, many different crops planted, sold nationally and internationally

#### POSSIBLE RESPONSE

Technology has radically changed food production methods in my country since the 1950s. Fifty years ago, any agricultural work involved heavy manual work for both men and women because of the lack of machinery. Also, back then, the harvested crop was mostly rice which was sold locally. Now, farms produce a range of crops and some of it is even sold on the international market.

**2** Are changes to food production methods that increase the quantity of food produced always positive?

#### IDEAS

lack of taste of mass produced food, increased amount of chemicals used

_____

**3** Compare the types of food consumed in your grandparents' time to the types of food you consume now.

#### IDEAS

_____

_____

**4** How will shopping for food change/evolve in the next few decades?

#### IDEAS

_____

_____

Check the Answer key for model answers to these questions.

## Clarification strategies

**READ ME** In Part 3, there is a possibility that you will be asked a question that you do not understand. Maybe the topic will be completely unknown to you or there will be a key word that you do not know. In this case don't panic. Instead clarify (make clear) what the examiner wants you to talk about.

There are several ways to do this. One way is to ask the examiner to rephrase the question in a different and/or simpler way. However, a more effective way would be to guess what the examiner is asking about and then use language to check whether your guess was correct. This will probably involve paraphrasing (putting in your own words) your understanding of the question you have been asked.

Here are two examples:

**EXAMPLES**

| | |
|---|---|
| Examiner: | Can you tell me what you think of government censorship of the media? |
| Candidate: | So, censorship is a type of control or restriction of the newspapers and magazines – is that right? |
| Examiner: | That's correct. |

| | |
|---|---|
| Examiner: | Tell me the main differences between the educational system in your country and the system in this country. |
| Candidate: | Ah – you'd like me to explain how education is organised in my country and then compare it to here? |
| Examiner: | Exactly. |

Other examples of phrases that introduce a paraphrase include: *So you're saying that …*; *Just to make sure I've got this right. Are you saying that …?*; *Alright, so you want me to …*

 3

---

### Exercise 9: Checking meaning

Listen to Part 3 from two sample IELTS interviews for the clarification strategies used by two candidates. In the table below, note down the words they use and whether they were successful or not.

| Speaker | How they ask for clarification | Successful? |
|---|---|---|
| Speaker 1 | Are you asking me about a city planning? | Yes |
| Speaker 2 | | |

Now check the Answer key to see an evaluation of their performance in this area.

---

### Thinking time techniques/fillers

Wherever possible, you should avoid silence in the Speaking Test. When faced with a difficult question or when you are searching for something to say, you can use a 'filler'; that is, a language technique that tells your listener you are organising your answer.

Examples of fillers include: *That's a difficult/interesting/complex question*; *Well, in my opinion …*

Another type of 'filler' are sounds such as *umm*, *ah* and *er*.

 4

---

### Exercise 10: Using thinking time strategies/fillers

Listen to Part 3 from two sample IELTS interviews. On the table below, note what thinking time strategies/fillers were used by the candidates. Were they successful or not?

| Speaker | Thinking time strategies/fillers used | Successful? |
|---------|--------------------------------------|-------------|
| Speaker 1 | Recent development? Let me see. Okay. | Partially successful |
| Speaker 2 | | |

Now check in the Answer key to see if your evaluation was correct.

---

### Exercise 11: Further practice for Part 3

With a partner, give extended answers to the questions below on education. Make sure that you use complex sentences and a variety of vocabulary in your answers. Don't forget to use clarification and 'thinking time' strategies where appropriate.

**1** Do you think computers will replace the majority of classroom teachers in the future?

**2** Has the standard of education changed for the better or worse in the past decade in your country?

**3** In your experience, do government or private schools prepare their students better for successful adult lives?

**4** What are the reasons behind the worldwide trend in most countries for students to continue into higher education after finishing school?

**5** Who do you think is primarily responsible for the development of children and teenagers into responsible adults?

**READ ME**

# 4 The speaking skills you need

In assessing your performance on the Speaking Test, the examiner considers your performance in four skill areas:

- speaking fluently and coherently

- using vocabulary effectively

- speaking accurately and appropriately

- speaking clearly.

The examiner awards a score in each of these four areas and then the four scores are averaged to give you your result for the Speaking Test. In this section we will look at each of the four skills in turn. In each of the four sections there are exercises that give you an opportunity to:

- listen to other people speaking in practice IELTS tests and assess their ability

- practise some of the speaking skills yourself

- do some IELTS-type tasks yourself and assess your own ability.

## ABILITY TO SPEAK FLUENTLY AND COHERENTLY

**READ ME**

The examiner awards a score from 1 to 9 for your 'fluency and coherence'.

## Speaking fluently

Speaking fluently means being able to speak smoothly and continuously. Of course it is normal and natural to pause sometimes when you speak, in order to think about what you are saying. If, however, you have frequent and lengthy silences, or if you keep repeating yourself and cannot continue speaking, then clearly you are having difficulty knowing what to say next, or how to say it. This will lower your score.

Speaking fluently does not mean speaking *quickly*. It is not realistic or necessary to try to speak as quickly in English as in your first language. Rather, aim to speak continuously and at a relaxed pace. The delivery should be smooth, not 'stop-start'.

Sometimes candidates hesitate too long because they don't know what to say next. If you find this happening, try one of the thinking time techniques discussed in Unit 2: 3. This will give you time to think and help you to keep going. Sometimes candidates hesitate too long because they don't know or can't remember the English word(s) they want to express their meaning. This happens especially when in their minds they are translating from their first language.

**EXAMPLE**

Candidate:   My country has very high … SILENCE … I don't know how to say.

In this example, the candidate does not speak fluently. He cannot think of the English word for inflation. Instead of hesitating and staying silent so long, the candidate should quickly avoid the problem and use words which he *does* know, and which give more or less the same meaning. For example:

**EXAMPLE**    Candidate:    My country has very high … the price of everything in my country goes up very quickly.

Here the candidate has repaired the problem by avoiding it. Familiar words are used with confidence and the same meaning is achieved.

Successful communicators are good at using what they know and avoiding what they don't know. They use other words to express their meaning.

---

### Exercise 12: Using other words to express meaning

For each of the following sentences, produce a sentence which expresses the same meaning *without* using the word(s) underlined. In some cases you might need two sentences to express the same meaning. The first has been done as an example. Make sure you do not hesitate too long. Keep speaking.

**1**   They postponed the meeting till Wednesday.
    *They changed the date of the meeting to Wednesday.*

**2**   My father retired a few years ago.

**3**   I do volunteer work in my spare time.

**4**   This dish is very nutritious.

**5**   She submitted her assignment on time.

**6**   There are many arguments in favour of teaching young children foreign languages.

**7**   Many people argue that television has a negative effect on children, but the evidence is inconclusive.

**8**   There has been widespread condemnation of the government's decision to amend the legislation without community consultation.

---

**READ ME**    Before you can judge your own ability to speak fluently, you need to be able to judge others' fluency. Exercise 13 will help you to do this.

**5**

---

### Exercise 13: Assessing fluency

Listen to two speakers in the practice Speaking Tests and decide which one is speaking more fluently.

**1** Listen to the tape and make your assessment.

**2** Listen again – this time reading the transcript at the same time – and check your assessment.

**3** Listen a third time and underline examples in the transcript which support your assessment.

**4** Check the assessment given in the Answer key.

In making your assessment, consider these issues:

- Do they speak smoothly and continuously?
- Do they speak at a reasonable pace?
- Are there many significant pauses?
- Are they able to 'fill' the pauses?

---

### Exercise 14: Speaking fluently

**A** Give extended answers to the following questions.

**1** Do you come from a large family?

**2** What do (did) your parents do for a living?

**3** Did (Do) your parents encourage you to get a good education?

**4** What are the main differences between education today and in your parents' time?

**5** How do you think schools will change in the future?

When answering try to speak as fluently as possible:

- Speak at a reasonable pace.
- Speak smoothly and continuously.
- Speak without too many (long) pauses.
- If you have pauses, try to 'fill' them.
- If you have any difficulty finding the word you want, use other similar words to express your meaning.

Record your answers and assess them for fluency. It is also useful to ask other people (study partners, teachers, native speakers) to assess your fluency.

**B** As a follow-up, answer all five questions together as a Part 2-type presentation. Speak for 1 to 2 minutes. Record your presentation and assess your fluency.

In Section 5 there are other suggestions for practising your fluency.

## Speaking coherently

READ ME

Speaking coherently means being able to speak in a clear and appropriate way. When you speak coherently, you make your meaning clear; that is, you present your ideas/information in a logical and clear sequence.

**EXAMPLES**

Examiner: Do you think boys are naturally better at mathematics than girls?

Candidate: Mathematics difficult girls clever boys good I think.

In this conversation, the candidate has not spoken coherently. The meaning is not clear.

Examiner: Where do you come from?

Candidate: I really like music.

In this conversation, the candidate has spoken accurately (the grammar is correct, for example), but has not spoken coherently. This answer does not make sense because it does not relate to the question. The answer is not relevant.

READ ME

In the following example from a practice IELTS Speaking Test, the candidate's answer is reasonably accurate but it is not coherent. It does not relate to the examiner's question. You can listen to the example on the tape.

 6

**EXAMPLE**

Examiner: In what way does a good system of public transportation affect the quality of life for city dwellers?

Candidate: Yeah. Public. Mm, public transportation? For the public buses I sometimes very confused to, how to use the buses and which bus is going which, ah, which place, you know. And so, how to pay a fee is different from the each cities. It's very confusing.

Candidates who speak coherently relate what they say to what the examiner says. It is a good idea to show this relationship explicitly. When answering questions in Part 1 and Part 3, for example, link your answers very directly to the examiner's questions.

**EXAMPLE**

Examiner: Did you know your housemates before you came here?

Candidate: No

The candidate's response gives the minimum connection to the question. The examiner cannot, however, be certain that the candidate has really understood the question.

If the candidate answers *No, I didn't*, the response is more coherent because it connects more directly to the question. It correctly follows the past tense used in the question.

If the candidate answers *No, I didn't know my housemates before I came here*, the answer is coherent because it repeats or 'echoes' the question.

If the candidate says *No, I didn't know them then*, then the answer is highly coherent. The candidate uses the pronoun 'them' to refer to the noun 'housemates' and uses the adverb 'then' to refer to the adverbial clause 'before I came here'.

Highly coherent communication uses such ways of referring to previous words. Rather than just repeating the question, it rephrases it (says it in a different way).

Here are some more examples from practice Speaking Tests.

**7**

**EXAMPLE**

| | |
|---|---|
| Examiner: | Okay. Why do you think some people are better at learning languages than other people? |
| Candidate: | Um, maybe they're very clever. (*laughs*) They're clever, there are a lot of people and, um, and maybe they work hard. |

This is a coherent answer. The speaker uses reference successfully, tying 'they' back to 'some people' in the question. The answer is also logical.

**8**

**EXAMPLE**

| | |
|---|---|
| Examiner: | Why do you think some people are better at learning languages than other people? |
| Candidate: | Ah, I think that some people do better in some languages because if the languages that they are studying has got, like, the same um, language structure, this will be much more easier for them to, to, um, handle with the language. |

This answer is coherent. The candidate echoes the question and thus ties the answer very directly to it. In repeating, she changes the words slightly, but this version is also correct. She then uses the link word 'because' to connect to a reason.

Now you can practise making *your* answers as coherent as possible.

---

### Exercise 15: Answering coherently

Respond to the following questions, making sure that you connect your answers very directly to the questions. Give both short and long answers, as in the example.

**1** Do you like your housemates

*Yes, I do. I like them very much.*

**2** Have you read the newspaper already?

**3** Have you ever been to Newcastle?

**4** Do you have ferries in your home town?

**5** Is there much crime in your home town?

---

**READ ME**  It is important to learn some of the standard ways of connecting answers to questions. For example, you should know how to respond when the examiner asks for your opinion. In Part 3 of the test you will often be asked your opinion.

**EXAMPLE**

| | |
|---|---|
| Examiner: | Do you think it will succeed? |
| Candidate: | Yes, I think so./No, I don't think so./I hope so./I hope not. |

## Exercise 16: Answering coherently

For each question below give two answers: a short answer; and a longer answer which connects very directly to the question. One has been done for you as an example.

**1** Do you think smoking should be banned in all restaurants?

*No, I don't think so. No, I don't think it should.*

**2** Do you think political leaders should be required to be university graduates?

**3** Do you think school children should have drug education?

**4** Do you think robots will replace teachers in the future?

**5** Should the genetic modification of food be allowed?

The following exercise provides further practice in answering coherently when you are asked your opinion.

## Exercise 17: Answering coherently

For each question below give two answers: a short answer; and a longer answer which connects very directly to the question. One has been done for you as an example.

**1** What do you think of the Internet?

*I love it. It's really useful and it's fun too.*

**2** How did you find your teachers at high school?

**3** How do you like living here?

**4** What do you think of action movies?

**5** What do you think of mobile telephones?

**6** What did you think of English when you first started learning it?

**READ ME**

Two further points about expressing your opinion:

Sometimes the examiner will ask your opinion with a 'how' question (that is, 'how' followed by an adjective or adverb). For example:

How important is good health in your opinion?

How difficult is it to find rental accommodation in your home town?

How strongly do people feel about the environment?

In order to give a coherent response to this question, you need to specify a degree in your answer. For example:

I think it is extremely important/quite important/very important/rather unimportant.

I don't think it's important at all.

A second point to remember is that a negative opinion may be structured differently in English to how it is in your language. In English the standard structure for a negative opinion is *I don't think he will come*, whereas in some languages the structure is *I think he will not come*. Make sure that you know how to express negative opinions.

---

### Exercise 18: Answering coherently

For each question below, give a very coherent answer by clearly specifying the degree. Then practise adding an extension to this statement (eg a positive or a negative opinion). The first two have been done for you as examples.

**1** How important is good health?

*It's extremely important. I don't think other things have any value without good health.*

**2** How difficult is it to get access to a computer at your university?

*It's not difficult at all actually. I don't think I've ever had any problems with access.*

**3** How widespread is the use of the Internet in your community?

**4** How common are mobile telephones in your country?

**5** How big a role does television play in your society?

**6** How important do you think it is to educate young children about drugs?

**7** How popular are American movies in your country?

**8** To what extent should governments censor the media?

---

In the following exercise you will practise judging how coherently candidates speak.

 9

---

### Exercise 19: Assessing coherence

Listen to two speakers. Decide which candidate answers more coherently. Use the following procedure:

- Listen to the tape and make your assessment.

- Listen again, this time reading the transcript at the same time, and check your assessment.

- Listen a third time and underline examples in the transcript which support your assessment.

- Check the assessment given in the Answer key.

In making your assessment, consider these issues:

- Is everything they say relevant to the questions?

- Do they echo or rephrase the questions?

- Do their answers follow the tense used in the question?

- Do the answers refer back to the question through using, for example, pronouns?

- Are the answers organised in a clear and logical sequence? Do the answers make sense?

In the following exercise you will practise speaking fluently and coherently.

---

### Exercise 20: Speaking fluently and coherently

**A** Answer the practice questions below. Make sure you give reasonably detailed answers to the questions. Simply answering 'yes' or 'no' is not enough. Record your answers.

#### Part 1-type questions

1 What's the climate like in your country?

2 What do you do in your spare time?

3 Do you have a Bachelor's degree?

4 Can you cook?

5 Are there private (non-government) schools in your country?

#### Part 3-type questions

6 Do you think anti-drug commercials on television help reduce the drug problem?

7 How important is it to have success in your career?

8 How hard should it be to get a driver's licence?

9 Do you think most children will study at home in the future?

10 Are computers really essential in education nowadays?

**B** Listen to your recordings and assess them for fluency and coherence. In particular:

- Do you speak at a reasonable pace?

- Do you keep pauses relatively brief (and fill them appropriately)?

- Does your way of speaking sound smooth?

- If you have difficulty finding the right words, do you use other words to express your meaning?

- Are your answers totally relevant to the question?

- Do your answers refer back very directly to the questions (for example, through reference pronouns)?

- Do your answers clearly show that you have understood the questions (by echoing or rephrasing them)?

It is also useful to ask other people (study partners, teachers, native speakers) to assess your fluency and coherence.

---

**READ ME** We have focused on *answering* coherently, but of course coherence is necessary at all times. In making the presentation in Part 2, for example, it is important to speak coherently; that is, to present information/ideas in a clear and logical sequence where the points are well linked. We look at linking ideas into complex sentences in 'Ability to speak accurately and appropriately' later in this section (see 'Grammatical range').

Coherent communication is well organised. In Part 2 you have a minute to organise what you are going to say and to make notes if you wish.

Throughout the other parts of the test you do not have any extra time to prepare what you are going to say. Nevertheless, it is a good idea to take a moment to consider what you are going to say. It is not necessary to reply immediately or to speak absolutely non-stop at all times. It is fine to pause and consider for a few seconds.

## ABILITY TO USE VOCABULARY EFFECTIVELY

**READ ME**

The examiner awards a score from 1 to 9 for your 'lexical resources'. 'Lexical resources' refers to your vocabulary; that is, your ability to:

- use a wide range of appropriate and accurate words when you speak

- use other words to express your meaning successfully when you lack some of the vocabulary usually used to convey that meaning.

### Accuracy and range of vocabulary
### Accuracy

**READ ME**

The 'accuracy' of your vocabulary refers to choosing the right words for the context. For example, the vocabulary in the following sentence contains inaccurate vocabulary:

**EXAMPLE**

I opened the television and listened to the news.

Here the accurate words would be 'turned on' or 'switched on', not 'opened'.

 **10**

**EXAMPLE**

| Examiner: | Well, what's the most popular region in your country for an overseas tourist if I was to come and visit? |
|---|---|
| Candidate: | I think in my country most people have no relig ... yeah? |

Here the candidate seems to confuse the words 'region' and 'religion'.

**READ ME**

The vocabulary you use in the test should also be *appropriate*. That is, it should be appropriate words for the situation, in this case a formal interview with an examiner. While greeting someone with an informal expression such as 'Hi' or 'G'day' might be appropriate in some situations in some countries (eg among friends in Canada or Australia), it is not appropriate in a formal interview (in that case, 'Hello'/'Good morning' etc would be more appropriate. Similarly, answering a question with 'Yeah' or 'Yep' (informal versions of 'yes') is not appropriate in a formal interview.

Also, the use of 'no problems' or 'no worries' in response to 'thank you' is not appropriate in this context. (If the examiner says 'thank you' at the end of the test, the most appropriate response from you is actually 'thank you'). The best way to learn more about the appropriateness of vocabulary is to read and listen to as much English as possible. Good dictionaries also tell you whether a word is informal or slang.

## Range

**READ ME**

The examiner will also consider the *range* of your vocabulary. Are you able to use a variety of different words, or do you always use a limited number of words again and again? You should try to demonstrate as much variety as possible. For example:

- when the examiner asks your opinion on different matters, don't *always* answer 'I think …'. Try other expressions, such as: *I feel/believe that …, As far as I can see/tell …, In my opinion …, I would say that …*

- when describing quantity, don't *always* use the same word, for example 'many'. Try other expressions, such as: *quite a lot of, a lot of, lots of, a large/huge/enormous amount/number of, the majority of*

- when describing what you like, don't *always* use 'I like…'. Try other expressions, such as: *I really enjoy…, I'm really keen on…, I'm fond of …, My favourite …*

- when describing the degree of something, don't *always* use 'very'. Try other expressions, such as: *extremely, somewhat, rather, quite, really.*

These various alternatives do not have exactly the same meaning. You need to check the differences in their meaning and usage and then use them appropriately.

---

### Exercise 21: Using a range of vocabulary

For each of the questions below, use as wide a range of vocabulary as possible to say the underlined answers in other ways. The first has been done for you as an example.

**1** Do you think schools should teach sex education?

<u>No, I don't</u>.

*No, I certainly don't.*
*No, I'm definitely not in favour of that.*
*No, I'm completely opposed to that idea.*

**2** Do you think sport should be compulsory at school?

<u>Yes, I do</u>.

**3** Do you have a lot of crime in your country?

<u>Yes, it's very bad</u>.

**4** Describe your apartment.

<u>It's very big and very nice</u>.

**5** How do you feel about smoking in restaurants?

<u>I think it should be banned</u>.

---

**READ ME**

When developing your vocabulary, it is useful to see the relationship between words. Are they related according to theme? Are they similar to other words? Are they opposite in meaning to other words? It is better to see words in the context of other words, not in isolation.

A wide range of vocabulary includes a command of common 'idioms'. An idiom occurs when two (or more) words are used together to form a new meaning; for example, 'to have a good time' which means to enjoy oneself. Many idioms are a combination of a verb and a preposition (this is sometimes called a 'phrasal verb'). For example, 'work out' is used in the meaning of 'succeed' in the sentence '*I started a new business, but it didn't work out*'. Similarly, 'pass away' means 'die' in the sentence *My grandmother passed away*. Section 5 has some suggestions for developing your knowledge of idioms.

Questions in Part 1 and Part 3, and the presentation topic in Part 2 are opportunities for you to display what you can do in English. This includes displaying the range of your vocabulary. Exercise 22 gives you practice in using a range of vocabulary.

## Exercise 22: Using a range of vocabulary

Below are some extracts from Part 1 and Part 3 of practice IELTS Speaking Tests. In each extract, respond to the examiner's two questions, making sure that your second response uses *different* vocabulary from your first response. Some have been done as examples.

**1** Examiner: Do you think voting should be compulsory?

Candidate: *Yes, I do. I feel that it's our obligation to vote.*

Examiner: So do you think people should be fined if they don't vote?

Candidate: *Yes, definitely. I really believe that the government should force people to vote.*

**2** Examiner: How does this city compare to your home town?

Candidate: *Well, it's much bigger and more expensive.*

Examiner: Are there any other differences?

Candidate: *Yes, there certainly are. My home town is far more beautiful.*

**3** Examiner: Are there many cinemas in your home town?

Candidate: *Oh, yes, there are a lot. People really enjoy going to the cinema.*

Examiner: And what about restaurants?

Candidate: _____

**4** Examiner: Do you think computers will replace traditional schools?

Candidate: *No, I don't think so. We'll always need teachers no matter what.*

Examiner: So will children study at home in future, do you think?

Candidate: _____

**5** Examiner: Do you find English more difficult than other foreign languages?

Candidate: _____

Examiner: And do you think the IELTS test is more difficult than other tests?

Candidate: _____

... continued over

... continued

**6** Examiner: Is studying at university harder than studying at high school?

Candidate: _____

Examiner: Is it more enjoyable?

Candidate: _____

**7** Examiner: Are mobile telephones common in your country?

Candidate: _____

Examiner: What about personal computers?

Candidate: _____

**8** Examiner: Are adults better at learning foreign languages than children?

Candidate: _____

Examiner: And are women better than men at learning foreign languages?

Candidate: _____

**9** Examiner: What's it like in the southern part of your country?

Candidate: _____

Examiner: And what's the northern part like?

Candidate: _____

**10** Examiner: Do you think primary school children should wear uniforms to school?

Candidate: _____

Examiner: What about high school? Should high school students wear uniforms?

Candidate: _____

 **11**

## Exercise 23: Assessing range of vocabulary

Listen to the two speakers and decide which one uses a wider and more effective range of vocabulary. Use the following procedure:

**1** Listen to the tape and make your assessment.

**2** Listen again, this time reading the transcript at the same time, and check your assessment.

**3** Listen a third time and underline examples in the transcript which support your assessment.

**4** Check the assessment given in the Answer key.

In making your assessment, consider these issues:

• Do they use a range of vocabulary in their descriptions?

• Where they give a number of opinions do they use different expressions?

• When describing quantity ('a lot') or degree ('very'), do they use a range of vocabulary?

## Paraphrasing

**READ ME**
The examiner will also judge your ability to paraphrase; that is, to express your meaning successfully even when you lack some of the vocabulary that otherwise might be used to convey that meaning. This is an important skill. If you can paraphrase, then you can maintain your fluency and successfully manage your communication. Below are some examples of paraphrasing by test candidates. You can listen to them on the tape.

**EXAMPLE**

| | |
|---|---|
| Candidate: | Um, I think security probably the major reason, ah, so if people who choose to live in the gated community, they probly, probably (oh, sorry, I have the problem with that word). They perhaps, the reason for them to choose is for the concern of security, as I just say earlier. |

In this example, the speaker explicitly declares her difficulty, namely that she is not confident that her pronunciation of 'probably' will be clear enough to be understood. So, she uses an alternative word ('perhaps') to express her meaning. Although it does not have exactly the same meaning, it is close enough, and it allows the speaker to keep going.

**EXAMPLE**

| | |
|---|---|
| Examiner: | Mm. What do you think is the most effective way to learn a language? |
| Candidate: | To practise, to use it, to – yep, just to use it, um, with the people from that language, from that culture. I think that's the best way. |

In this example, the speaker begins to select a third verb after 'To *practise*, to *use it*' (maybe she intended something like 'to try it out'). However, she strikes some difficulty in deciding what the word(s) should be and so instead she recycles one of the previous words and gives it an appropriate emphasis by adding 'just'. In this way she is able to keep going and make her communication successful.

---

### Exercise 24: Assessing the ability to paraphrase

**1** Listen to the speaker and answer this question:

Does the speaker paraphrase?

**2** Listen again, this time reading the transcript as you listen.

What do you think the speaker wants to say? What words could she use to express this meaning?

---

You have already practised paraphrasing in Section 4 'The speaking skills you need' (Exercise 12). Below is another exercise to practise this skill.

---

### Exercise 25: Paraphrasing

Read out each of the sentences below, but replace the underlined words with *other* words that have the same meaning. Do not hesitate too long in thinking of the alternative words. The first one has been done as an example.

**1**   I have a driver's licence but <u>it's not valid</u> here in Canada.

*I have a driver's licence but it is not accepted here in Canada.*

**2**   People who <u>are highly motivated</u> are generally more successful.

**3**   I really feel that countries should <u>cooperate</u> more. If we don't, then <u>global warming is going to get much worse</u>.

**4**   I couldn't finish my assignment in time so I <u>requested an extension</u>.

**5**   I think newspaper reports <u>are more reliable than</u> news reports on television.

---

**READ ME**    Now focus on your own vocabulary. In the next exercise your aim is to use vocabulary which is accurate, appropriate, and varied. You also should concentrate on paraphrasing where necessary.

---

### Exercise 26: Using vocabulary effectively

**1**   Below are three practice topics for a Part 2 presentation. For each topic take one minute to prepare what you are going to say. Record your presentation.

    **A**   Talk about your best friend. Who is it? How do you know each other? Why are you such good friends?

    **B**   Talk about a song which you think is typical of your country. What is it about? Why is it typical? How do people in your country feel about this song?

    **C**   Choose a sport which you find enjoyable. Do you watch it or play it? Why do you enjoy it? What skills does this sport require?

**2**   Now listen to your recorded presentations and assess them from the perspective of vocabulary. In particular:

Are your words accurate (that is, they have the right meaning in this context)?

Are your words appropriate (that is, they are suitably formal for an examination/ interview)?

Do you use a reasonable range of words (avoiding repeated use of the same simple words such as 'I think' or 'I like' or 'very good', etc)?

It is also useful to ask other people (study partners, teachers, native speakers) to assess your vocabulary.

---

## ABILITY TO SPEAK ACCURATELY AND APPROPRIATELY

**READ ME**    The examiner awards a score from 1 to 9 for your 'grammatical accuracy and range'.

### Grammatical accuracy

Grammatical accuracy simply means using grammar correctly. For example, the examiner assesses whether you follow the standard patterns for sentence structure (word order), verb tense, (modal) auxiliary verbs, number (singular/plural), articles, and so on.

**EXAMPLE**

Candidate 1: In my apartment have two bedroom and one bathroom. It really comfortable, but expensive. I live there for seven month now. It locate near university. I can to walk there just five minute.

Candidate 2: There are three bedrooms and two bathrooms in my apartment. It's rather small, but very convenient. I've been living there for three months. It's located very close to my college so I can walk there in about ten minutes.

The first candidate does not use plural nouns accurately ('bedroom', 'month' and 'minute' should all be plural). The structure to express the existence of something – one of the most basic tasks in giving a description – is also not used accurately; the form should be either *In my apartment there are two bedrooms* or *My apartment has two bedrooms*. The use of tense is inaccurate in 'I live', and the modal auxiliary verb 'can' should not be followed by 'to'. By contrast, the second candidate uses accurate grammar.

**READ ME**    Improving the accuracy of your grammar is one way of preparing for the Speaking Test. The best way to do this is to identify your weaknesses and develop a program of practice (see Unit 2: 5). It is not possible to predict precisely which structures you will need to use in the Speaking Test, but it is reasonable to expect at least the following:

- describing things (places, buildings, food) and people: *there is/are*; nouns (singular/plural forms); passive forms of the verb (eg 'it was built in 1900')

- describing events in the past: past tense and present perfect tense

- describing aspects of your life: simple present tense

- talking about plans: future tense/present continuous tense

- comparing things: comparatives/superlatives

- expressing opinions: modal auxiliary verbs

- discussing hypothetical situations: conditionals (especially 'first' and 'second' conditionals)

You need to be able to use these structures accurately, although of course you do not need to know the correct grammatical terms for them. Unit 2: 5 will suggest ways to check (and enhance) your competence in using correct grammatical terms.

**15**

## Exercise 27: Assessing grammatical accuracy

Listen to the two speakers in the practice tests and decide which performance is more grammatically accurate. Use the following procedure:

**1** Listen to the tape and make your assessment.

**2** Listen again, this time reading the transcript at the same time, and check your assessment.

**3** Listen a third time and underline examples in the transcript which support your assessment.

**4 Check the assessment given in the Answer key.**

When making your assessment, consider how successfully the candidates have used these structures:

> there is/are/was/were
>
> singular/plural forms of nouns
>
> passive forms of the verb
>
> past tense and present perfect tense
>
> simple present tense
>
> future tense/present continuous tense
>
> comparatives/superlatives
>
> modal auxiliary verbs
>
> conditionals.

For further practice, correct the grammatical errors you find in both transcripts, and then check the Answer key again.

**READ ME**    In the IELTS Speaking Test you are judged for your grammatical *performance*, not your grammatical *knowledge*. It is not enough to know the correct forms: you must produce them consistently when you speak – forming tenses accurately, remembering to add plural endings on nouns when needed, forming the passive voice correctly, and so on. Your aim throughout is to keep grammatical errors to an absolute minimum.

## Exercise 28: Speaking with accurate grammar

Give full (extended) answers to each of the following typical questions of Part 1 of the Speaking Test. Record your answers and then assess their grammatical accuracy by referring to the Answer key.

1 What did you do in your spare time when you were a child?

2 Which did you find more enjoyable – primary school or secondary school?

3 What kind of films do you like best?

4 Who are better drivers – men or women?

5 What do people do during (the most important festival in your country)?

6 How did you feel when you graduated from high school?

7 Have you ever taken the IELTS test or the TOEFL test?

8 How would you spend your money if you won the lottery?

9 Who was your favourite teacher at high school? Why?

10 How many foreign countries have you been to in your life so far?

11 Describe your best friend to me.

12 Which do you find easier to understand – American English or British English? Why?

13 What advice would you give to a young friend hoping to study overseas?

14 How long have you been studying English?

15 Approximately how many universities are there in your country?

16 How many hours per day do you usually sleep?

17 Describe a famous building in your country.

18 When is your birthday? How do you usually celebrate it?

19 What part of your country would you recommend every visitor to see?

20 Do you think that cash (that is, paper money and coins) will disappear in the future?

## Exercise 29: Speaking with accurate grammar

Here are some notes about the life of a writer.

**A** Read the notes and then answer questions 1 to 15 below.

Francis James Hatton

born Newcastle 1967

only child; abandoned by parents; raised by grandmother

extremely poor; worked part time (after school)

attended local school until 1982

worked in department store until 1987

short story ('Black Morning') published 1987

three more short stories published 1988

quit work to write full time

novel (*This Man*) published 1988

novel (*Eternity*) published 1990

1991: sold film rights to *Eternity* for $1.5 million

Academy Award (Best Screenplay) 1993

married Elizabeth Charles 1995

daughter Clara born 1997

son Andrew born 1998

daughter May born 2000

current residence: Monaco

current project: a collection of short stories about his childhood

  **1** What is his full name?
    *His full name is Francis James Hatton.*

  **2** Why was he raised by his grandmother?

  **3** Why did he work part time?

  **4** How old was he when he left school?

  **5** How many novels has he published?

  **6** Has he ever published any short stories?

  **7** How did he earn $1.5 million?

  **8** When did he win an Academy Award?

  **9** Who(m) did he marry?

**10** How old was he when he got married?

**11** How many daughters does he have?

... continued over

... continued

**12** Who is older – Clara or May?

**13** Where does he live?

**14** What is he working on at the moment?

**15** How many siblings does he have?

**B** Now use the notes to give a full biographical description of Frank Hatton. Record your description and then compare it with the version in the Answer key.

**C** As a follow-up, give a spoken biography of a famous writer in your country, a friend, and yourself.

## Exercise 30: Speaking with accurate grammar

Look at 1 to 6 below and describe in detail what you see. Record your descriptions and then check the Answer key. The first one has been done as an example.

**1**

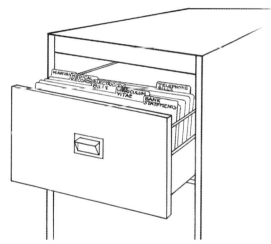

There are six files in this drawer. (This drawer has/holds/contains six files). Each file has a label. The files are arranged alphabetically (in alphabetical order). The files include personal items such as curriculum vitae and household items such as telephone bills.

To make your answer grammatically correct, it is essential that the plural form 'six files' is clear and the existential form (*there* + verb: *to be*) is constructed correctly – in this case 'there are'. If an alternative structure is used (such as 'this drawer has/holds/contains ...) then the present tense verb must show that the subject is third person singular.

**2**

... continued over

… continued

**3**

**4**

**5**

## Grammatical range

READ ME Your grammatical range is also assessed when you speak. The examiner judges whether your structures are sufficiently complex and diverse.

**EXAMPLE** Candidate 1: In a city, the transportation is very important. I think the government should spend, should pay more attention to the education. Mm, and, um, let the people know how

FOCUSING ON IELTS: LISTENING AND SPEAKING SKILLS

to be a good person, how to live in their modern city. Yeah, ah, the spirit is very important. People must to learn.

Candidate 2: I think a good transportation system will bring a great deal of convenience for people because if there is no traffic jam, people can save a lot of time and they can walk everywhere more easily. You will become angry waiting and waiting, especially when you meet with a traffic jam, and sometimes it takes you so much time. If you have a good transportation system, you can go everywhere. All the people benefit and the streets are better.

In this example, the first candidate's grammar is quite accurate, but very limited in range, using only simple sentences (single-clause sentences with only one verb or verb group). The second candidate uses a wider range of grammar. The structures connect points in an efficient and clear way and are more diverse, including compound and complex sentences (sentences that contain two or more verbs or verb groups).

**READ ME**     You can research the difference between complex and compound sentences by looking at grammar reference books, but it is not essential for you to understand the distinction. What is important is your ability to connect points of information accurately, which is the focus of the next exercise.

### Exercise 31: Speaking with appropriate grammatical range

For each item below, continue the simple sentence to make at least two compound sentences and/or complex sentences. You can do this by, for example, linking it to other information, giving a reason, adding some detail, or expressing a contrast. The first has been done as an example.

| **1** I'm planning to study French | (link to other information) *and go to France.* <br><br> (give a reason) *because I feel it will be useful.* <br><br> (add detail) *which I think is a beautiful language.* <br><br> (express a contrast) *though I'm not very good at languages.* |
|---|---|
| **2** I enjoy living in a small town | |
| **3** I think we should reduce the number of cars in our cities | |
| **4** I have never used the Internet | |
| **5** We need to focus on improving the health of our children | |

**READ ME**    Questions in Part 1 and Part 3 and the presentation prompts in Part 2 provide you with an opportunity to display your grammatical range.

- 'Why' questions can often give you an opportunity to produce complex sentences giving reasons; for example: *I consider him a great teacher because he's able to inspire students.*

- 'When' questions might give you an opportunity to produce complex sentences such as: *I met him at university when we both joined the chess club.*

- 'How long' questions might give you a chance to produce complex sentences such as: *I've been collecting stamps since I was about five years old.*

- Questions asking you to describe or assess something/somebody might enable you to produce compound sentences; for example: *My course is quite difficult but I really enjoy it.*

- Questions asking your opinions could allow you to produce complex sentences such as *I really feel that it should be banned.*

- Questions asking you to specify (Which?/What kind?) can give you an opportunity to produce complex sentences such as: I *like books that make you think about life.*

- Questions asking about goal or purpose might give you an opportunity to produce complex sentences such as: *I'm doing this degree so that I can learn how to manage my own business in the future.*

---

### Exercise 32: Using a range of grammatical structures

**A** Answer questions 1 to 10 below. In your answers, focus on achieving accurate and appropriate compound/complex sentences. Then check the sample answers in the Answer key.

**1** How long have you been studying English?

**2** Why do you want to study at a foreign university?

**3** What's your house (apartment) like?

**4** Do you enjoy speaking English?

**5** What kind of people do you like?

**6** Should university education be free?

**7** At what age do men usually get married in your country?

**8** Why do so many people choose to learn English as a foreign language?

**9** Do you read the newspaper every day?

**10** Why are you taking this test?

... continued over

... continued

**B** Items 11 and 12 are sample Part 2 cards. Respond to each card under test conditions, giving yourself one minute to prepare and then speaking for 1 to 2 minutes. Record and transcribe your presentations.

**11**

> **CANDIDATE'S CARD**
>
> Describe your best friend.
>
> Say:  who it is
>
> how long you have known each other
>
> where you met
>
> Explain why you regard this person as your best friend.

**12**

> **CANDIDATE'S CARD**
>
> Describe a film you have enjoyed watching.
>
> Say:  what the name of the film is
>
> what the film is about
>
> how it differs from other films
>
> Explain why you consider this film so good.

**C** Listen to your recording and read your transcript to assess the grammatical range. Have you taken enough opportunities to achieve compound/complex sentences? Have you produced the structures accurately?

Compare your answers with the sample answers in the Answer key.

 **16**

## Exercise 33: Assessing grammatical range

Listen to the two speakers and decide which speaker uses a wider range of structures. Use the following procedure:

**1** Listen to the tape and make your assessment.

**2** Listen again, this time reading the transcript at the same time, and check your assessment.

**3** Listen a third time and underline examples in the transcript which support your assessment.

**4** Check the assessment given in the Answer key.

In making your assessment, consider whether there is a mix of simple, compound, and complex sentences.

## Exercise 34: Speaking with accurate and appropriate grammar

You have just interviewed two candidates for the position of receptionist in a hotel catering to French and German tourists. Here are the notes you made during the interviews.

| JACK | PATRICK |
|---|---|
| well dressed/groomed | well dressed; grooming and posture poor |
| nervous | confident |
| French ✓  German ✓ | French ✓  German rusty |
| not able to answer question re customer complaints | able to answer all questions |
| immature | very mature(?) |

Use the notes to give a verbal report to your supervisor about each candidate.

As a further step, make a recommendation to your boss. Which person should be recruited? Why?

Record what you say and then assess it for grammatical accuracy and range. Check the Answer key.

## Exercise 35: Speaking with accurate and appropriate grammar

1   Below are some Part 3-type questions. Respond immediately to each question and record your answer.

   A   If you could, how would you change the education system in your country?

   B   In your view what are the characteristics of a good friend?

   C   Do you think that there should be a minimum age and a maximum age for politicians?

2   Now listen to your recorded answers and assess them from the perspective of 'speaking accurately and appropriately'. To help you assess more carefully, you may find it useful to write down (transcribe) what you have said. Check the following:

   • Is the grammar associated with your nouns correct; for example, articles, number (singular/plural), adjectives, comparative and superlative forms of adjectives, relative clauses?

   • Is the grammar associated with your verbs correct; for example, tense, subject-verb agreement, negative forms, modal auxiliary verbs, adverbs, adverbial clauses?

   • Do you use *there is/are/was/were* correctly?

… continued over

... continued

- Are your prepositions correct?

- Do you use conditionals correctly?

- Do you use a range of sentence structures (ie compound or complex sentences as well as simple sentences)?

It is also useful to ask other people (study partners, teachers, native speakers) to assess your grammatical accuracy and range.

## ABILITY TO SPEAK CLEARLY

**READ ME**     In the IELTS Speaking Test, 'speaking clearly' refers to your pronunciation. Specifically, you are assessed on your:

- production of individual sounds

- correct word and sentence stress

- focus stress on information words

- linking between words

- use of rhythm (stress timing)

- use of intonation and pitch.

This section will deal with active use of these aspects of pronunciation.

Throughout the Speaking Test the examiner listens to your pronunciation and decides whether it is native speaker like (a band 8), satisfactory (band 6), below average (band 4) or extremely poor (band 2). This abbreviated four-point scale applies only to pronunciation. Specifically, the examiner will grade your performance based on three main criteria:

- the amount of effort he/she has to put into understanding your speech

- how much of your speech is lost due to poor pronunciation

- the effect of first language interference on your pronunciation.

 17

---

### Exercise 36: Assessing pronunciation

Listen to the two speakers in the practice Speaking Tests and decide which one is speaking more clearly. Use the following procedure:

1   Listen to the tape and make your assessment.

2   Listen again, this time reading the transcript at the same time, and check your assessment.

3   Listen a third time and underline examples in the transcript which support your assessment.

4   Check the assessment given in the Answer key.

---

## Production of individual sounds in English

If you have learned English as a second language, your production of individual sounds – as well as other aspects of your pronunciation – will rarely be completely native speaker like. Your first language will always affect the way you pronounce sounds (phonemes). In most cases this is not a major problem as non-native speakers can usually communicate well with an approximation of English sounds. However, some learners of English have problems producing in English particular sounds that do not occur in their first language. For example, many Thai English language learners have trouble with the sound /θ/ as they are unfamiliar with this sound in their own language.

 18

---

### Exercise 37: Recognising problems with individual sounds

Listen to Part 2 of the IELTS Speaking Test. What sounds does the speaker have particular problems with? How do her problems affect her speech?

Now read a discussion of her performance in the Answer key.

---

One way to identify and work on problems with individual sounds is to use a phonetic chart/script. This is a special alphabet for pronunciation that has one symbol representing each phoneme in the language. These charts are usually divided into vowels (a, e, i, o, u), diphthongs (a combination of two vowel sounds) and consonants (all other sounds in English).

---

### Exercise 38: Practising individual sounds

Get a copy of the phonemic chart from your dictionary or another source. Try to get a version using the variety of English you wish to speak (Australian English, Canadian English etc). Work with another learner of the same language background and agree on a list of sounds that cause problems for speakers of your language. Practise these 'problem sounds' – first in isolation and then as they occur in words. Practise some of the sounds every day until you are more confident.

---

## Word stress

When a word has more than one syllable, one syllable usually carries the main stress or accent. For example, the first syllable of the word _telephone_ is stressed while in _become_ the second syllable is stressed and in _automatic_ the third. Stress is demonstrated by either saying the stressed syllable a little louder and/or holding it a little longer. Unstressed syllables are short and often have a reduced vowel sound.

The best way to get to know the stress patterns of individual words is to note the individual stress markings for words shown in your dictionary and to listen carefully to native speakers.

**19**

---

### Exercise 39: Recognising word stress

Read the following passage and underline where you think the word stress on all words of two or more syllables should go. The first sentence has been marked for you as an example.

<u>Wel</u>come to the phe<u>nom</u>enon that is the Con<u>ven</u>ience Store. First launched in Australia by the *7–11* company in 1977, these abbreviated supermarkets of the late twentieth century continue to expand at an incredible rate. Once inside, it's the brightness that registers first. An explosion of massed fluorescent tubes assaulting your eyeballs with pure white light.
As your eyes gradually adjust, your sense of nutritional balance is next challenged – with sugar or salt the principal ingredient of almost everything around you. Tightly wrapped in plastic, the displayed goods are unified only in their distance from nature. Vegetables and loaves of brown bread are a rarity but artificially flavoured confectionery and gigantic muffins are ready and waiting for your custom.

Now check your answers by listening to the passage as it is read by a native speaker. Then compare your version with the Answer key.

---

## Sentence stress (including focus stress)

**READ ME**    English speakers often give more or less prominence to particular words in a sentence. This is because stressed words – sometimes called content words – usually give important or new information to the listener while unstressed words simply join information together or provide less important information. If you give all the words you use equal stress, a native speaker listening to you may misunderstand what you mean or they may miss the most important information.

**20**

### Exercise 40: Recognising sentence stress (including focus stress)

Listen to these five examples of the same sentence said with different sentence stress. Underline the word in the sentence that is stressed and carries the focus. What does the speaker want the listener to focus on in each sentence? The first one has been done for you as an example.

**1** Could <u>you</u> help me with my preparation for the IELTS exam?

Focus:    *The speaker wants to focus on the listener rather than anyone else as a possible provider of help.*

**2** Could you help me with my preparation for the IELTS exam?

Focus:    The speaker wants to _____

**3** Could you help me with my preparation for the IELTS exam?

Focus:    The speaker wants to _____

**4** Could you help me with my preparation for the IELTS exam?

Focus:    The speaker wants to _____

**5** Could you help me with my preparation for the IELTS exam?

Focus:    The speaker wants to _____

Now check your answers in the Answer key and practise saying the sentences with different sentence stress.

**21**

### Exercise 41: Practising sentence stress (including focus stress)

Listen to the following monologue twice. For the first time just listen and read. The second time you listen, underline the words you think have been stressed by the speaker. Why have they been stressed? The first sentence has been done for you as an example.

<u>King</u> Street, the main street of <u>Newtown</u>, is <u>the</u> place to go for <u>lunch</u> when you're looking for a <u>break</u> from the frenetic pace of <u>shopping</u>. I'd recommend RooBar for its food. It's been established a long time and is undoubtedly the most stylish café on King Street. Their menu is wonderful especially their all day breakfast of eggs, tomato and sausage on bread for only $5.90. What a bargain! Also, for vegetarians, their extensive non-meat menu includes such delights as scrambled tofu or banana bread.

Check your answers in the Answer key and practise the monologue with special attention to focus stress.

### Linking

**READ ME**    Native English speakers do not usually pause between each word they say, rather they glide smoothly from one word to the next. Joining words together is called linking and occurs naturally in rapid, spontaneous speech. Linking occurs when the sound at the end of one word joins together with the sound at the beginning of the next word. Normally, linking happens automatically but it can be consciously exaggerated when speakers want to skip quickly over less important information. It can also disappear altogether when a speaker wants the listener to focus on one particular piece of information.

 22

## Exercise 42: Recognising and practising linking

Listen and read the following sentences. The second time you listen, mark words that are linked to other words. The first sentence has been done for you as an example.

1   I am sick of listening to that terrible banging noise.

2   Who's going to the movies tonight?

3   What are you doing on the weekend?

4   I thought you said you were going to do the washing up.

5   Switch on the light. How often do I have to tell you?

6   The lecture, given by Professor Adams, was highly entertaining.

7   The weather'll be cool and cloudy for the remainder of the week.

Check your identification of linking with the Answer key. When you've finished, practise saying the sentences with a partner, paying special attention to linking.

## English rhythm (stress timing)

**READ ME**

Rhythm is part of the music of language – specifically it is the beat of the language. Rhythm results from the pattern of stressed and unstressed syllables in speech. English is a stress-timed language, which means that strongly stressed words (normally content words such as nouns or verbs) drive the rhythm and occupy most of the speaker's time and effort. Weakly stressed words (such as prepositions, articles and pronouns) are generally delivered rapidly in the time between the strongly stressed words.

The way you pause (the amount of stops or breaks in your speech) affects your rhythm in English. Pausing can help listeners distinguish between important information and background information and can also give dramatic impact to speech. However, if you pause too often – for example between most words – your English rhythm will be disrupted and your listener may find it uncomfortable to listen to you for long periods.

**23**

### Exercise 43: Recognising English rhythm (stress timing)

Listen to two extracts from Part 2 of the Speaking Test. While you listen, note which speaker delivers their talk with a more noticeable English rhythm and who uses more pauses in their speech.

Check your evaluation with a discussion of their performance in the Answer key.

 **24**

### Exercise 44: Practising English rhythm

This exercise will help you with your rhythm.

**1** Imagine you are at a party and are being introduced to several people. Listen to the example and note how English rhythm is based on stressed syllables rather than on every syllable.

 **a** *I'd like you to meet Geoff, Lynn an(d) Mark.*

 The three names all have only one syllable and they are the only stressed words in the sentence. Listen to what happens when the names become longer than one syllable.

 **b** *I'd like you to meet Howard, Catherine an(d) Melinda.*

 You will have noticed that the beat of the sentence remained the same even though the names got longer. Sentences A and B are both said in approximately the same amount of time.

**2** Now try a similar exercise with a partner using the following structure:

 *Hello, my name is (your name) and this is (name), (name) and (name).*

 Before you start, mark the predicted stress pattern of the names you will say.

 Nicholas, Rosemary, Jill

 Margaret, Jaclyn, Andrew

 Yvette, Paul, Valerie

 Rowena, Colin, Sharon

 Lincoln, James, Alexandra

Source: This exercise was adapted from an idea by M Vaughan-Rees 1992. 'Approaches to pronunciation teaching'. *Review of ELT* 2, 2: 48

## Intonation and pitch

**READ ME**    English speakers change the pitch of their voices as they speak, sometimes making it higher and sometimes lower. This rising and falling melody is called intonation. Movement in pitch can be sudden or gradual and can be put together in various tone combinations. In the IELTS Speaking Test, you are expected to use intonation and pitch to help you send precise messages about what you mean, or to reinforce a message.

In Exercise 45 you will consider the example of the word 'Tuesday'. The word only has one meaning, but the use of different tones can greatly alter its significance.

 25

---

### Exercise 45: Recognising intonation and pitch

Listen to five ways 'Tuesday' is said and then match them with the interpretations below. The first one has been done for you as an example.

| | | | |
|---|---|---|---|
| **1** Tuesday | | **A** | Rise-fall to indicate surprise |
| **2** Tuesday | | **B** | Falling tone to indicate a statement |
| **3** Tuesday | | **C** | Strongly rising tone to indicate a question |
| **4** Tuesday | | **D** | Low rise tone to indicate incomplete information |
| **5** Tuesday | | **E** | Fall-rise tone to indicate hesitation or uncertainty |

---

Specific functions of English tones include:

1   Level or low rise tone:   incomplete, of minor importance

2   High or rising tone:   used for yes/no and clarification questions

3   Falling tone:   used for 'wh-' questions, commands or statements

4   Fall-rise tone:   to show uncertainty, hesitation or contrast

5   Rise-fall tone:   used for exclamation/surprise and displaying a strong attitude towards a subject

 26

---

### Exercise 46: Analysing intonation and pitch

Listen to a part of the candidate's talk and read about the intonation and other pronunciation features she has used.

Examiner:   Why did you choose this particular course?

(LEVEL TONE)

Candidate:   Um, because, ah, when I was teaching and I thought I should learn

(SLIGHT FALL)

something more about the linguistics, and that's why I, I chose this, um,

area to study.

Intonation used:   The answer to this question is said at a low, level tone. A slight fall occurs when the speaker makes her final statement on the question (Function 1).

Other features:   Sentence stress on the words 'teaching', 'learn' and 'linguistics'.

… continued over

---

... continued

Now listen to a few more sentences and note how the candidate has used intonation and other pronunciation features.

**A** Examiner: Mm, what are the most challenging or difficult things about your course?

Candidate: Well, I think the most difficult part is the reading part, because um, quite a lot of a new concepts involved in, and ah, that the things I didn't know before. So I think that's the most difficult part for me.

Intonation used:_____

Other features: _____

**B** Examiner: And what will you do when your course finishes?

Candidate: Um, teaching, I guess. I would go back and I'm still, I'm doing teaching and I will ... I would prefer actually, prefer to use the knowledge I learned here, so back to teaching again.

Intonation used:_____

Other features: _____

Now check your evaluation with the Answer key.

# 5 Developing your study program

To prepare for the IELTS Speaking Test, you need to devise a study program that will help you develop your strategies and skills.

- First decide what your needs are.

- Then choose some materials to practise your speaking.

- Then practise the strategies and skills required by the Speaking Test.

## DECIDING YOUR NEEDS

**READ ME**

Think about what you need. For example, do you need to focus on improving your pronunciation? Do you need to practise presenting your ideas? Do you need to check your understanding of what is in the IELTS Speaking Test? Complete the following checklist to help you think about your needs. Tick the items that you need to work on in your study program.

| Speaking checklist | ( ✓ ) |
|---|---|
| **Which aspects of the IELTS Speaking Test do you need to check?** | |
| the length of the test | ( ) |
| the number of parts in the test | ( ) |
| what is expected of you in each part | ( ) |
| the types of topics there might be in each part | ( ) |
| the kind of information on the card which the examiner gives you | ( ) |
| the instructions the examiner will give you | ( ) |
| how long you must speak in the second part | ( ) |
| how you are assessed by the examiner | ( ) |
| **Which speaking strategies do you need to improve?** | |
| answering questions about familiar topics | ( ) |
| giving a short presentation | ( ) |
| structuring and organising a presentation | ( ) |
| noting down ideas for a presentation | ( ) |
| participating in a more abstract discussion | ( ) |
| extending your answers | ( ) |
| using clarification strategies | ( ) |
| using 'thinking time' techniques and 'fillers' | ( ) |

… continued over

… continued

**Which speaking skills do you need to improve?**

| | |
|---|---|
| speaking fluently | ( ) |
| speaking coherently | ( ) |
| learning new vocabulary | ( ) |
| using other words to express your meaning | ( ) |
| using vocabulary accurately and effectively | ( ) |
| using a range of vocabulary when you speak | ( ) |
| paraphrasing when you speak | ( ) |
| speaking with accurate grammar | ( ) |
| speaking with an appropriate range of grammar | ( ) |
| pronouncing individual sounds correctly | ( ) |
| using word stress appropriately | ( ) |
| using sentence stress appropriately | ( ) |
| linking sounds appropriately | ( ) |
| speaking with appropriate (stress-timed) rhythm | ( ) |
| speaking with appropriate intonation | ( ) |

## FINDING APPROPRIATE MATERIALS TO PRACTISE SPEAKING

**READ ME**  Your first resource is the tape accompanying this book. Do all the exercises on the tape as you read through the unit. Consider the practice tests in Unit 2: 6 as model speaking interviews, and especially note the strategies the candidates use to answer difficult questions.

Here are some other possible resources:

### English-language radio and television stations

Try finding national and international English-language radio and television stations. Listen to them as much as you can and record important programs so you can play them back for possible transcription and more detailed practice. If you want to practise your awareness of pronunciation, don't listen so much for content – rather listen to the sounds and 'flow' of the language.

### Websites

Do a search for relevant websites on the Internet. Use a reliable search engine like Google (www.google.com) or Mamma (www.mamma.com) to discover IELTS speaking practice resources in cyberspace. In particular, you can find some good pronunciation sites on the Web. Do a search under English language pronunciation to see what you can find.

## Textbooks and audio-visual resources

Textbooks and audio-visual resources are a good source of material for structured speaking practice. Choose material that practises the skills that you identified in the checklist as needing work.

Suggested textbooks and other resources are listed here according to the different skills assessed in the Speaking Test. Some have accompanying cassettes.

For a general introduction to the area of improving your speaking (and other skills) independently, the following resource is highly recommended:

Ellis, G and B Sinclair 1989. *Learning to learn English: A course in learner training.* Cambridge: Cambridge University Press

## Speaking fluently and coherently

Please note that resources in this section marked with * focus on giving presentations, which is most useful for Part 2 of the IELTS Speaking Test.

Collie, J and S Slater 1993. *Speaking 4.* Cambridge: Cambridge University Press

Comfort, J 1995. *Effective presentations.* Oxford: Oxford University Press*

Ellis, M 1992. *Giving presentations.* Harlow: Longman*

Geddes, M 1991. *Advanced conversation.* London: Macmillan

Ryan, K 2000. *Speaking and debating with style.* Victoria: Phoenix Education

Watcyn-Jones, P 1997. *Pairwork 2 (intermediate to upper-intermediate).* Harmondsworth: Penguin Books

## Using vocabulary effectively

Your first resource for vocabulary practice is a good, advanced level English-English dictionary such as the *Oxford advanced learner's dictionary* or the *Collins COBUILD English language dictionary*.

Please note: In this section textbooks to help build up your general vocabulary in lexical areas which are likely to occur in the IELTS test are marked with *.

Blundell, J 1982. *Function in English.* Oxford: Oxford University Press

Gough, C 2001. *English vocabulary organiser.* Hove: Language Teaching Publications*

Harrison, M 1991. *Word perfect: Vocabulary for fluency.* Surrey: Nelson*

Keller, E and S Warner 1988. *Conversation gambits.* Hove: Language Teaching Publications

McCarthy, M and F O'Dell 1994. *English vocabulary in use.* Cambridge: Cambridge University Press*

Thomas, B J 1989. *Advanced vocabulary and idiom.* Walton on Thames: Longman*

Wellman, G 1992. *Heinemann English word-builder.* Oxford: Heinemann*

## Speaking accurately and appropriately

Please note: Resources in this section which give grammar rules and also exercises at an IELTS level are marked with *.

Eastwood, J 1999. *Oxford practice grammar*. Oxford: Oxford University Press*

Fitikides, T J 2000. *Common mistakes in English*. Harlow: Longman

Hewings, M 1999. *Advanced grammar in use*. Cambridge: Cambridge University Press

Swan, M 1995. *Practical English usage*. Oxford: Oxford University Press

Swan, M and C Walter 1987. *How English works*. Oxford: Oxford University Press*

Willis, D 1991. *Collins COBUILD student's grammar*. London: Harper Collins*

## Speaking clearly

All the materials in this section focus on practising pronunciation and all are accompanied by a cassette. Those that concentrate on sounds in English are marked with *.

Aiken, G and M Pearce 1993. *The sounds of English*. Sydney: Blackfriars Press*

Bradford, B 1988. *Intonation in context*. Cambridge: Cambridge University Press

Brazil, D 1994. *Pronunciation for advanced learners of English*. Cambridge: Cambridge University Press

O'Connor, J and C Fletcher 1989. *Sounds English*. Harlow: Longman*

Rogerson, P and J Gilbert 1990. *Speaking clearly*. Cambridge: Cambridge University Press

Zawadzki, H 1994. *In tempo: An English pronunciation course*. Sydney: NCELTR, Macquarie University

## PRACTISING THE STRATEGIES AND SKILLS NEEDED FOR THE SPEAKING TEST
### Exercises for independent study
### Find speaking models

**READ ME**

You need to collect as many speaking 'models' as possible on audiotape and videotape. Models are examples of good speaking (either by native speakers or competent non-native speakers). Even if you can't record and re-play them, you should listen to as many models as you can (while sitting on the bus, listening to the radio, and so on).

By listening to models carefully (focusing on their pronunciation, their fluency, their vocabulary, and so on), you can increase your awareness of your own speaking targets.

### Practise speaking with other people

To reach your speaking targets, you need to speak in as many authentic situations as you can find every day. If you live in an English-speaking country it should be relatively easy for you to find situations in which to practise your English.

Finding situations to practise the more structured presentational style English of Part 2 of the Speaking Test is more difficult; however, you could join an organisation such as 'Toastmasters' or even start your own speaking group for further practice in this area.

## Practise speaking by yourself

Even when you don't have anyone to speak with, you can still have a regular program of independent speaking practice. It is important to find a regular time to work on your speaking and to practise as much as you can.

First you need to build up a stock of practice questions. There are sample Part 1, 2 and 3 questions throughout Unit 2: 4 and Unit 2: 5. You will also need to generate your own questions. You can look at the resources suggested above (see pages 100–2) to help you produce questions. You can look at your photo albums and your CV to think of Part 1 questions, and look at television, radio, and books to help you think of Part 2 and Part 3 questions.

Write each question on a separate card or piece of paper, and mix them all together in a container. Then, at regular times in your study schedule, select a question from your container to practise.

Record your performance. If possible, videotape it.

Listen to the recordings and judge them according to the IELTS assessment criteria discussed in Unit 2: 4. Assess just one criterion each time you listen. Then use your self-assessment to decide what your main needs are. Adjust your study plan accordingly.

If possible, keep all of your recordings and note the date on each. Later you can listen to older recordings and notice how your performance has changed (eg I am more relaxed now, my pronunciation is better, my structure is more accurate). Assessing your progress over time will motivate you to keep practising. Improving your speaking skills is a matter of regular long-term practice.

## Speaking fluently and coherently

When you listen to models, focus on how fluently they speak. Notice how they maintain their pace of speaking. Notice any techniques they use to gain 'thinking time'. Notice how, if they cannot find a particular word to express their meaning, they find other words and thus keep the conversation or presentation flowing smoothly.

You may find it useful to repeat particular sentences that you have selected from the recorded models. Say these sentences as fluently as you can, then record your versions and compare them to the models.

When you are involved in authentic conversations (or presentations) try to focus on your fluency. Keep speaking as smoothly as you can and, for this practice, be less concerned about the accuracy of what you say. Make sure that, above all, you do not stop communicating simply because you cannot find a particular word. Quickly find a different way to say it and keep going. Don't try to translate word for word from your native language.

You should also listen to your models from the perspective of speaking coherently. Pay particular attention to how the speakers relate their answers to the questions. Notice, for example, how they use pronouns to refer to nouns in the questions (eg Q: Do you think cash will disappear in the future? A: Well, I think *it* will be used less often, but I don't think *it* will entirely disappear).

When you are involved in authentic conversations, pay particular attention to answering questions very coherently. Make it very clear that you have understood the question and, above all, make sure that your answers are completely relevant. If the question asks you why, make sure your answer gives a reason. If the question asks for a description of something, make sure you describe it.

When you select from the stock of questions in your independent study program, record your performances and then assess them for their coherence. Check whether your answers to Part 1 and 3 questions are clearly tied to the questions. When you listen to your Part 2 presentations check them for relevance. Is everything you say related to the topic? If necessary, amend your answers and presentations and record them again.

## Using vocabulary effectively

When you listen to your models, focus on the vocabulary the speakers use when they communicate. Decide if you think the words you hear are useful for your goals. If they are, try to use them yourself when you have conversations or when you are practising speaking at home in your study program.

When you are having conversations with people, take note of the vocabulary that people use. Don't hesitate to ask people the meaning of the words they use and what words you could use to express the meaning you want to convey.

Also, when you are involved in authentic conversations, try to vary your vocabulary as much as possible. For example, don't *always* say 'How are you?', 'I'm majoring in chemistry', and so on. Find other ways of saying these things (eg 'How's your day been?', 'My main subject is chemistry'). Make diversity your goal.

When you record your speaking performances at home, write down what you said. Go through these transcripts and underline the main content words. Assess your vocabulary from the perspective of accuracy and then range. Ask a fluent speaker to assess your vocabulary as well. Use a dictionary or thesaurus to explore synonyms that you could have used.

Vocabulary development should be an ongoing thread in your study plan. Look again at 'Using vocabulary effectively' in Section 4 and pay particular attention to how to select and memorise new words. Collect all of your new vocabulary together, in a notebook, for example, so that you can learn new words easily. This way, you can also see how much you have achieved and you will feel positive about your progress.

The best way to organise your vocabulary notebook is by theme or category, for example:

- words that describe emotions
- words connected with the university
- words describing towns/cities
- words describing houses/apartments/buildings

- words about the media
- words describing transport
- words describing festivals and customs in my country
- words connected with expressing opinions
- words to express likes/dislikes/preferences.

Organising in this way will help you remember the words and also help you see synonyms, so that you can make your vocabulary as varied as possible.

Vocabulary development needs to be ongoing, regular and structured. Set yourself a target, for example, five new words every day.

## Speaking accurately and appropriately

When listening to your models, focus on the speakers' grammar. The best way to do this is to look at transcripts of their speaking as you listen. Each time you listen and/or read, adopt a different focus; for example, 'This time I'll listen to all of the nouns and pay attention to singular or plural','This time I'll listen to all the tenses', and so on. It will also be easier to assess the structural *range*, if you use a transcript.

It is important, also, to listen to recordings of your own practice answers and presentations. Again, transcribe exactly what you said, and analyse it for grammatical accuracy. Ask someone else to check your assessment. Identify your problem areas in grammar. Make a shortlist of your priority grammar weaknesses and then gradually work on improving them. Use grammar resources that both explain grammar rules and have grammar exercises to practise (see the list of resources earlier in this section). Good dictionaries can also help with clear grammar models.

Another way to assess your grammatical accuracy is to locate and use grammar tests, for example multiple-choice questions or gap fill tests. Analyse your errors to pinpoint problems in your command of English grammar.

Also assess your transcripts for their grammatical *range*. Does your speaking show a range of simple and complex sentences? When you want to extend your Part 1 and Part 3 answers, or when you are making a Part 2 presentation, try to make one point and then immediately link it to another related point (by, for example, adding a detail, a reason, or a contrast). This should help you to form more complex structures.

As well as listening to your models, you can develop your structural accuracy and range in the long term by *reading* and *writing* as much as possible. The skills of listening, reading, writing and speaking are interrelated.

## Speaking clearly

Carry a notebook around with you and note down different ways of expressing things when you hear them. This could be anything which interests you and which will help you with forming natural structures and building your vocabulary. Also note down the *way* people say things – the stressed words, use of rhythm and intonation, etc. For several days afterwards, try to use what you have learnt in your daily speech.

If you are speaking with a native speaker, ask them to check your pronunciation and give you feedback. Also notice when a native speaker misunderstands you or asks you to repeat yourself. This may be caused by particular aspects of your pronunciation, and should be noted in your notebook.

Your main priority is to determine your target – what specific aspects of your pronunciation do you need to improve? Check your notebook. Make sure you find out which English sounds or clusters tend to give difficulty to speakers of your first native language. (A 'cluster' is a combination of sounds such as links and asks.) Listen to recordings of yourself speaking (either in authentic situations or in your practice program at home answering your stock of IELTS-type questions). Assess your pronunciation of individual sounds and clusters. Listen to your stress (both word stress and sentence stress), your intonation and your rhythm. Ask other people, particularly native speakers, to assess your speaking.

Once you have identified your priorities, you will know what to practise. Choose one particular part of the day and work systematically through your priorities. Here are some of the specific techniques you can use when practising:

- Get a list of words containing your difficulties (ie sounds and clusters which you find difficult to pronounce or words with stress patterns which you find difficult to produce), and practise saying them aloud on a regular basis.

  As you practise, speak slowly and carefully (it is not necessary to speak as quickly as a native speaker). A good way to practise is to regularly pronounce all English vowels, consonants and diphthongs using a phonemic chart. Vowel sounds are particularly important, so exaggerate the movements your mouth and jaw make so that each one is clearly defined. When practising, it is important to use a good English-English dictionary, or even a pronunciation dictionary so that you can be sure you are following accurate models of pronunciation.

- To practise your intonation, experiment with varying your intonation and note the effect it has on the message you are giving out. Repeat the same sentence with completely varied intonation; for example, try to sound interested/bored, kind/cruel, friendly/unfriendly. Ask a native speaker to listen to a recording of your different sentences and tell you how you sound.

- Talk aloud to yourself as a rehearsal for spoken language. Doing this will force you to predict all the important pronunciation features of words and sentences and it will give you confidence when you later produce the language 'for real'.

- Shadow reading can also help you in preparing for spoken language. This involves reading aloud with a recorded speaker on a tape/CD, following the pace, rhythm and intonation of the original speaker. This can help with pronunciation and also with fluency and cohesion.

- Practise projecting your voice, so that the examiner does not have to strain to hear you. When you listen to recordings of yourself speaking, can your voice be easily heard? Keep practising until your voice is sufficiently loud.

## Exercises for study partners

Having a study partner to practise English with can enable your English to improve rapidly. If possible, choose a partner at the same English language level – possibly someone in the same class who wants to do the IELTS test at the same time as you do. It would be a good idea if this person spoke a different first language from you, so you can work solely in English.

## Just a minute or two

This is an activity which improves fluency. Choose one of the following topics or choose one of your own. Then talk for one to two minutes on the topic without any repetition or long hesitations. If your partner notices any repetition, hesitation or simply can't understand what you're saying, they should say 'stop' and then you should start again. Once you have successfully finished, it is your partner's turn to speak about another topic.

### *Possible topics*

| | |
|---|---|
| Refugees | Something that scares me |
| My favourite restaurant | Dangerous games |
| Developments in personal communication | The last book I enjoyed |
| A perfect weekend | Technology and education |
| Student fees | An interesting person I've met in the last week |
| My best travel experience | Diet and health |
| Noise pollution | A person I really admire |

You can adapt the game to focus on other aspects of speaking; for example, say 'stop' when you hear a grammar mistake or a pronunciation error, and so on.

## Reading aloud

Read aloud to your study partner. As this involves reading to an audience, you will need to incorporate all the features of delivering a presentation. Read the text first and mark it up with word and sentence stress before you begin. While doing this, try to hear the sound in your head before you make it with your voice.

## An oral summary from a written text

Both of you read the same short passage from a magazine/newspaper, then think about how you would summarise it orally to an audience. Remember that written English is different to spoken English, so you will have to change the vocabulary and make it simpler so your 'audience' can digest it. If possible, get another person to listen to both of you deliver your talks so he/she can say which one was more successful and why. Do this with different texts, explaining the text to your partner.

## Practising English sounds

This is best done with three or four other people. Each person has to write ten sentences using minimal pairs; for example, 'I lost my pack/pick'. The writers then mark the word in each pair that they intend to pronounce. Writers then read their sentences out loud and the other group members have to write the word they hear. If the listeners are unable to detect accurately which word the writer said, it may be because the word was mispronounced.

# 6 IELTS practice test: Speaking

A complete practice Speaking Test has been provided for you on the tape accompanying this book. It has been written to simulate the IELTS Speaking Test in its style, format, and length. The practice test has been administered twice so that you can listen to and compare two candidates taking the test.

**READ ME**

You have two options in using this practice test. If you have a study partner to help you, you could take the practice test yourself before you listen to the models. If you do not have a study partner, you can listen to the two candidates and assess their performance.

## DOING THE PRACTICE SPEAKING TEST YOURSELF

**READ ME**

If you would like to use the tests for active practice, ask a study partner to read the transcript so he/she knows how the interview is conducted. Then ask the study partner to note down suitable questions and to take the role of the examiner. You should simulate the conditions of the test by sitting opposite each other at a desk and by using a tape recorder to record the test. Make sure that you follow the time guidelines for each part. The 'examiner' will need to use a watch to ensure the guidelines are followed.

When you finish, listen to the recording. Assess your own performance, paying particular attention to your ability to speak fluently, coherently and clearly, and to your use of vocabulary and structure. Then ask your study partner to assess your performance. Once you have finished, you can listen to the two candidates on the tape and assess their performance.

## ASSESSING OTHER CANDIDATES DOING THE IELTS PRACTICE SPEAKING TEST

**READ ME**

For each candidate, listen to the tape right through without reading anything or making notes. As you listen, make a general assessment of the candidate's performance, focusing on their ability to speak fluently, coherently, and clearly, and on their use of vocabulary and structure.

Then listen to the tape again, this time reading the transcript as you listen. This will help you to understand more clearly what the candidate and examiner are saying. You will then be able to confirm (or change) your initial assessment.

Listen to the tape for a third time, and again read the transcript as you listen, but this time underline examples which support your assessment. Finally, check the Answer key to compare your assessment.

# Transcripts

## UNIT 1: LISTENING

### Examples page 5

**Listen carefully and answer questions 1 to 2.**

 **1**

A: Morning. Can I help you?

B: Hi. Yes. I'm thinking about buying a computer. Do you sell second-hand computers? You know, computers that have been reconditioned so they're like new again.

A: No, we find there's a limited market for them, to be honest. We only sell new computers here. Brand-new.

B: OK. Well, let's have a look.

A: Sure.

B: Oh, and what about renting? Do you rent computers at all?

A: No, we don't rent, I'm afraid.

B: OK.

A: You might be surprised how good the prices are these days, though.

B: I hope so.

A: OK. What kind of computer? Desktop or laptop?

B: Laptop. I want to be able to take it with me to the university. I've got a desktop at home, but it's really old and I can only use it when I'm there.

A: And you wouldn't consider a palmtop, you know, like one of these small ones that you can hold in the palm of your hand?

B: No, I don't think so. I want a proper keyboard.

**Listen carefully and answer questions 3 to 4.**

A: OK. A laptop. Well, they're the most popular these days.

B: Really?

A: Yes, we sell more laptops than desktops and palmtops combined.

B: I guess that's not surprising.

A: And what are you going to use your computer for? You have to think about your specific needs.

B: Well, mainly word processing, I guess.

A: OK. Anything else? Internet, games, graphics?

B: Yeah, all those things sometimes, I guess. But most of the time I just use it for word processing.

A: Well you can get all of those functions easily with any of these laptops.

**Listen carefully and answer questions 5 to 6.**

B: OK. Great. How heavy are laptops anyway?

A: They're really light nowadays. Here, hold this one.

B: Yes, I see what you mean. It's really light. Incredible.

A: Of course, you'll generally find that the really light laptops are more expensive than the heavier ones.

B: I see.

A: This one, for example, the Apex. It's by far the lightest of the three laptops we sell, and that's why it's the most expensive.

## Listen carefully and answer questions 7 to 8.

B: I should write all this down. So, what have we got? Apex, Sunray, and Nu-tech. And how much do they weigh?

A: The Apex is 1.9 kilograms …

B: 1.9.

A: … the Sunray is 2.4 kilograms

B: 2.4.

A: And the Nu-tech is the heaviest at 3.1.

B: 3.1. And what are the main differences between them?

A: Well, you'd have to say that the Apex is the most convenient, because of its light weight. If, like you said, you're going to carry it around a lot, to and from university, that might be a factor for you. The Sunray, on the other hand, is the most powerful, there's no doubt about that.

B: So, it will handle the Internet fine?

A: Sure. It's well named. It's like the sun, really powerful. It'll handle all your needs. And the Nu-tech is the cheapest, which …

B: … which could also be a factor.

A: Yes.

## Listen carefully and answer questions 9 to 10.

B: I like the look of the Sunray.

A: Yes, I do too.

B: And what are all these?

A: Well, here on the left-hand side is the in-built CD-drive.

B: The what?

A: You know, the place to put your CDs.

B: Oh yes. I'm with you.

A: You just press here.

B: Yes.

A: And over on this side is the floppy drive … and this is the microphone.

B: Microphone?

A: Yes, if you want to record something on to your computer

B: Where? Here?

A: No, that's the ON/OFF button … Here next to it , you see the microphone?

B: Oh, yeah

A: And the mouse, of course

B: So, the Sunray has a mouse.

A: Yes, just like a desktop computer.

**Listen carefully and answer questions 11 to 13.**

B: Do all the laptops use a mouse?

A: No. There are different types. If you look here, you can see that the Apex has a touch pad … see, you just move your finger over this area here and that moves the cursor in the direction you want.

B: That looks pretty easy.

A: And the other type is a ball. You can see one on the Nu-tech here. You just move the ball like this.

B: I'm not so keen on that type. … Hmmm

**Listen carefully and answer questions 14 to 16.**

B: And tell me, what happens if there are problems with the computers – do they have a guarantee?

A: Oh, yes all of these three models have guarantees. The Apex and the Sunray are guaranteed for 12 months and the Nu-tech for 6 months. You can see it here on the labels. I suppose the Apex gives you the best arrangement, though, because it guarantees both parts and labour.

B: What do you mean?

A: Well, they will cover the cost of any parts in the computer that need to be changed, and also their labour – their time in fixing it – is covered. You don't have to pay anything.

B: Oh, I see.

A: But the Sunray guarantees parts only.

B: Parts only? Oh, I see. I would have to pay for the labour.

A: Exactly. And the Nu-tech is the same as the Sunray.

B: OK. Right. That's great. Well, I think that'll do for the moment. Thanks very much.

 2

## Exercise 1

A: Have you finished your assignment?

B: Almost. I'll be finished tomorrow.

A: That's a relief.

B: Actually, I really enjoyed this assignment, to tell the truth.

A: How come?

B: It was interesting. I'd never thought about all this stuff.

A: Like what?

B: Well, like all of the data on gender. Did you know that females make up 52% of university students? Who would have expected that? I was sure that there would be more males than females at university.

A: Yes, me too. That's great.

B: Yes, well it's not all great. Things are very different at the top, believe me. Do you know how many female Vice-Chancellors there are in the entire country?

A: No idea.

B: Guess.

A: Ten?

B: Three!

A: That's not very good, is it. Anyway. Your assignment looks good. Very impressive.

B: I still haven't done the references. Once they're done, it'll be finished.

A: I hate doing the references too.

 **3**

## Exercise 2

A daring daylight robbery has stunned the small community of Roseville. At nine o'clock this morning, just after opening, two men wearing face masks entered the Central Bank and brandished shotguns. The terrified staff handed over the money, and the robbers fled the bank. Fortunately, there were no customers in the bank at the time. The robbers made their getaway in a blue Toyota sedan, driven by a third person. Bank officials have yet to confirm the amount of money stolen, but it is understood that the thieves may have got away with close to half a million dollars.

The two suspects are described as being in their late teens or early twenties, both of slim build and approximately 175cm tall. There is no description of the driver, although one witness has suggested that this person may have been a woman. This is the first major robbery in the small fishing-industry township and residents are extremely upset. The manager of the Central Bank, Elaine West, has announced that the bank will conduct a comprehensive and immediate review of its security procedures. If anyone has any information possibly relating to the robbery, please call the police hotline on 9357799.

 **4**

## Example page 10

A: Have you seen our new lecturer?

B: No.

A: That's her over there.

B: Gee, she's tall.

A: Don't worry about her height. Let's just hope she's a good lecturer.

 **5**

## Exercise 3b

A: I'm glad that's over.

B: What did they give you, Helen? Show me. Mmm. Until December, so that's – what? 9 months. That's good.

A: Well, I'm a bit disappointed, actually. I was hoping for 12 months.

B: I think 9 months is pretty standard for a student visa, though.

A: I guess so. Speaking of 12 months I wish I were in your situation, Mister 'temporary resident'.

B: And I wish I could turn that into permanent residence, so it's all relative.

 **6**

## Exercise 4

Now, before you go, let me give you the details of your next assignment. Yes, I know you're busy studying for your exams, but this is the last essay for the semester – and it has to be done. I've written the topic on the board. Can you all see it? Please copy it down and please make sure that you get it right. 'Attitudes towards public transport'. Now, as you can see, it's a very straight-forward topic and you shouldn't have too many difficulties with it. And you'll be happy to hear that it doesn't have to be very long. Ten pages. That's all, OK? Don't give me less than that and please don't give me more. Remember: I don't want a postcard and I don't want a thesis. As for methodology, well, I'm going to leave that open to you to choose. You can conduct a telephone survey, for example, or maybe a series of face-to-face interviews, or maybe you can do an in-depth case study and draw your conclusions from that. It's up to you, but please do think about it carefully before you decide which way to go. Now, you haven't got a huge amount of time to get this in to me. I want it submitted to me by the 11th of September. Is that clear? The 11th of September. And, as usual, I won't consider any extensions unless there are really exceptional circum-stances. Now, please also make a note of a few more points. As you know from before, it's an absolute requirement that the essay be word processed. No options here, I'm afraid. I don't want to be sitting up all night trying to decode your handwriting. Also, there must be a title page. Some of you failed to do this last time, so please make a note of it to remind yourself this time. And finally, please make sure that you include a statement of your methodology. Clear and concise, no more than say half a page. OK, That's about it. Any questions?

 **7**

## Exercise 5

(S = Speaker; R = Recording; M = Mia; O = Operator)

S: You're going to listen to a telephone conversation. Mia is telephoning an airline company. She wants to change her flight reservation.

R: Welcome to Sky Air, the friendly airline. If you would like flight arrival information, press 1. If you would like to make a domestic reservation, press 2. Please note that it is not necessary to confirm domestic flights. If you would like to make an international reservation, press 3. If you would like to speak to one of our sales officers, please hold the line.

M: Hm. Number 3, I guess.

R: You have reached international reservations. All of our operators are busy at the moment. Please hold and an operator will be with you as soon as possible.

M: Oh, come on. I'm in a hurry.

O: Good morning. Andrew speaking. Welcome to Sky Air. How can I help you?

M: Yes, I'd like to change my reservation, please. I can't travel on the day I booked. I have to work.

O: And what was your name, please, madam?

M: Mia Torres. T-o-r-r-e-s.

O: And what was the flight number, Ms Torres?

M: Yes, I have it here. SA233.

O: And do you have the date?

M: Uh … January 21st.

O: Right. I have it here. Sydney to Honolulu.

M: Yes, that's right.

O: Now, what would you like to change it to?

M: Well, what's available? Is there a flight on the 22nd?

O: No, I'm afraid not. There are only three flights a week direct to Honolulu. Mondays, Thursdays, and Fridays.

M: What time does the Friday flight leave?

O: All the flights leave at the same time – 5.45pm.

M: OK. Well, I'll take Friday the 25th. Do you have seats available?

O: Yes, we do. Would you still like a window seat?

M: Yes, please. I like sitting near the window – you can see everything.

O: OK. That's fine. Friday the 25th. The same flight number as before: SA233. And please remember to be at the airport two hours prior to departure.

M: Do I have to ring again and reconfirm?

O: No, Ms Torres. There's no need to reconfirm.

M: And I'd like to know … how much luggage can I take on the flight?

O: The allowance is 22 kilos.

M: So, if I have more than that I have to pay extra, right?

O: Yes, that's right. … So, can I help you with anything else?

M: Um … let me think … I wanted to change the date of my reservation … ask about re-confirming … and check the regulations about the luggage allowance … They were the main things, I think.

 8

## Exercise 6

A: Good morning. Ace Security. Can I help you?

B: Yes, I'd like some information about the alarm system in this house. I've just moved in and I don't know how to use it. The previous owner left me a code number, but that's about all I know about it. I've got no experience with using alarms.

A: Sure. Can you see the monitor on the wall?

B: Yes, I'm looking at it right now.

A: Good. What does it say on the screen?

B: 'Disarmed. Ready to arm.' Whatever that means.

A: Well, to arm is to 'activate', to 'switch on', I suppose.

B: So, disarmed means 'deactivated', I guess.

A: Yes, that's right.

B: Fair enough. So, how do I arm it then?

A: Well, you mentioned that you have a code, right?

B: Yes.

A: A four-digit number, right?

B: That's right.

A: Well, all you have to do is enter that code number on the key pad and press 'away'.

B: What does 'away' mean in this case?

A: It simply means 'go out', as in you want to go out of the house and therefore you want to activate the alarm system while you're away.

B: OK. I see. I thought it meant something like wipe it away. OK, so that's when I want to go out. What about when I come back into the house? Do I press the key with 'C' on it?

B: No. Actually, you enter your code again and press the 'off" button. Can you see it on the left hand side of the pad?

B: Oh, yes. So what is the 'C' button then, on the far right? I though it was 'c' for 'clear' like you get on a calculator.

A: No, actually it stands for 'change code'. That's the key you press when you want to change your four-digit code. For security reasons, for example.

B: Oh, I see. Well, I really had that one wrong. … So, OK. What's the asterisk just below it? Is that for emergencies or something?

A: No. That's what we call the 'fault check'. When you press that, the screen will tell you if there are any faults in the circuit, you know, faults as in 'problems', like you've left a window open somewhere or there's a problem with one of the sensors, for example, anything that needs to be checked before you're ready to arm.

B: Oh, I see. I guess it's not that complicated.

 **9**

## Exercise 7

To illustrate this phenomenon, let us look at a practical example. I'm sure you will have noticed that nowadays competitive swimmers typically wear full-length body suits, from neck to ankles, instead of the traditional briefs. Why do they do that? It certainly has nothing to do with appearance. In fact, some people don't like the look of them at all. Rather, the reason they wear these swimsuits is a matter of physics, and hence of interest to us in this course. The suits you see are specifically designed to improve performance by reducing drag.

Drag, of course, refers to contact which slows down forward movement. The issue of drag is important in many sports, including speed skating, cycling, and running.

Sports scientists have long worked on reducing drag by getting swimmers to shave their bodies. In experiments conducted in 1990 – you can follow up these experiments in the reading I've assigned for next week – in these experiments, they found that swimmers consumed something like 10% less oxygen after they shaved their body hair. The experiment was limited to shaving body hair, not head hair, although some studies conducted the following year also had similar results. Of course the experiments do not prove that shaving body hair will automatically help people swim faster, but it is clear evidence of the impact of reducing drag.

Scientists have extended their concern with drag in swimming even further and have collaborated with swimsuit manufacturers to produce a swimsuit which is like a new skin for the swimmer. They've done this by emulating the skin of one of the swimming superstars of the world, one of the fastest swimmers in the world – the shark. The new swimsuits are usually called 'shark-skin suits' because, of course, that's exactly what they look like – shark skin.

Sharks are a miracle of evolution who have ensured their survival by becoming faster swimmers than their prey or competition. But why are sharks so fast? Quite simply, because of tiny ridges all over their skin. Even though their skin looks remarkably smooth, their skin is, in actual fact, covered with these almost invisible ridges. And that is what the manufacturers have managed to put on the swimsuits – tiny ridges. And it's these ridges which reduce drag and help the swimmer glide through the water faster. At least, that is the theory. It is impossible to prove scientifically that these suits lead to better performance, and indeed some commentators are sceptical.

 **10**

## Exercise 8

**Tutor:** OK. We've looked at the issue of the quality of our politicians and you've all been rather critical of their performance. So how can we as a country improve the quality of our politicians? Do you have any practical suggestions? Yes, Mark?

**Mark:** Well, I really feel that politicians should be required to have a certain level of education.

**Tutor:** And what level of education would you require?

**Mark:** Well, at least a university degree.

**Sally:** I can't see the sense in that, I'm afraid.

**Tutor:** Why not, Sally? What's wrong with the idea?

**Sally:** Well, I don't think there's any evidence that university graduates are actually any better than less well-educated politicians. I mean, what's the connection between a university education and the quality of political leadership? We need politicians with good hearts, and good ethics, not clever brains.

**Anna:** I can't see any connection either. I mean, I don't feel any more intelligent now that I'm studying at university.

| Tutor: | Well, I'm not sure that intelligence is the issue, Anna. |
| John: | Exactly. It's not about intelligence. |
| Tutor: | Would you care to elaborate, John? |
| John: | University graduates have analytical skills and are better able to distinguish between facts and opinions, and that's really important, I think. Having those kinds of skills can't possibly hurt, and it might actually help raise the quality. I reckon we should make it a requirement. Some of our politicians are really pathetic. |
| Sally: | Well, I certainly agree with that. They're totally out of touch. Just dead wood. I reckon we should get younger politicians, not better educated ones. |
| Tutor: | You think we should have younger politicians, Sally? |
| Sally: | Yes |
| Anna: | No way. I think it's the other way round. We should put a minimum age requirement on people running for political office. We need people with more maturity, more life experience. Not younger people. |
| Tutor: | And what minimum would you suggest, Anna? |
| Anna: | Forty, I think. |
| John: | That sounds reasonable to me. |
| Tutor: | What about you, Mark? Do you agree? Is establishing an age requirement one way of improving the situation? |
| Mark: | Not as far as I can see. You're not going to get better politicians by worrying about their age. I don't know. Maybe the only way to get better quality is to pay more. Give politicians higher salaries and you'll attract better candidates. |
| Sally: | You're joking! |

## 11   Exercise 9

As the train slows to enter the station on this clear Friday morning, I'm suddenly aware of the huge central bank building. Its twin, thirty-nine metre towers and giant central dome momentarily overshadow the train's passengers. Why am I doing this? I think to myself as I prepare to leave my seat.

## 12   Exercise 10

The last decade of the twentieth century witnessed an explosion of interest in the field of travel writing. Bookshops that once had shelves stocked only with atlases, guidebooks and maps now include sections devoted to narrative and other personal accounts of travel. So why the massive growth in this type of travel writing? Some would give credit to a number of authors who have re-invigorated travel writing, with readers enthusiastically responding to their entertaining and often humorous style. But to my mind, the main aim of travel writing is to break the barrier of print and time and to make destinations alive in the mind of the reader.

## Exercise 11

So, I ask again, why this growth in travel writing? Is it because of these wonderful authors who have re-invented a tired genre? Or is there another reason? I would explain the popularity of the new travel writing as caused by the ever-expanding sameness and uniformity of the world. Nowadays, people find it harder and harder even to find, let alone travel to unusual places themselves, so they want to read about others doing it. Or, if the writing is about a familiar place, they may want to read how it's been given a new or unusual twist by a talented author.

This year I'm studying chemistry – in fact I've

just bought the main textbook – and physics.

## Exercise 12

Good morning class. Today, I'd like to talk about producing educational multi-media. This particular type of multimedia – as distinct from entertainment multimedia – is an area of interest for educators everywhere. I'd particularly like to discuss the process of producing this type of multimedia. Your first consideration, apart from deciding what medium you're going to deliver your product through, is your audience. Who they are, what they expect and, most importantly, what they need. After you have determined this basic information about your users, then you can go on to the all important area of content.

I think we're ready. We've got pens, pencils, erasers, and a stapler.

## Exercise 13

1   Cacti are part of a group of plants called succulents …
2   I'd like you to meet my friend, Vanessa …
3   We have a wide variety of language courses including Arabic, Tagalog, Thai …
4   Educational multimedia can be delivered via CD-ROM or over the Internet.
5   Flight number 823 from Kuala Lumpur is delayed …
6   I'd like to speak to the Managing Director, please.

## Exercise 14

Now he works as a tutor in molecular science at one of the local colleges. Apparently he earns around 50 per cent more than he used to. The workload is relatively heavy, but he has a reasonable amount of annual vacation. By and large, he's satisfied with his new position.

## Exercise 16

1   A:  Do you like my new radio?
     B:  Yeah, it looks great.
     A:  Actually, it's not a 'new' radio. It's an antique.
     B:  I love the colour. What's it made of?
     A:  Bakelite.

2   A:  Look, Jane. Isn't Dr Metwali great with kids?
     B:  Yes, kids adore her. Look at them all crowding around her. Mind you, it's no wonder.

**A:** What do you mean it's no wonder?

**B:** Well, she is a pediatrician, after all.

**A:** Is she? Someone told me she was a surgeon.

**B:** No, she's definitely a pediatrician.

**A:** Well, as you said, no wonder. I really admire pediatricians.

**B:** Why?

**A:** Well, it must be terribly hard for them, treating little kids who are seriously ill, you know, with terminal cancer or something.

**B:** Yes, I know what you mean. That must be hard.

**3 A:** Turn that radio off, will you. It's driving me crazy.

**B:** Don't you like the music?

**A:** No, it's not the music.

**B:** It's all the ads, with all those dreadful jingles. I can't bear them. I can't get them out of my head.

**A:** Well, all stations have ads, so you can't escape them. Anyway, jingles are music.

**B:** Please don't call jingles music.

**4 A:** The former Senior Accountant at Universal Machines, Alicia Trent, has been found guilty of embezzlement and has been sentenced to four years jail.

**5 A:** What a beautiful garden!

**B:** Thanks. Yes, it's coming along quite well. There's still a lot of work to do, though.

**A:** Like what?

**B:** Well, this wall for example. It's totally bare. I'm going to put a trellis here and I'm thinking of planting an allamanda.

**A:** That'd be nice. The yellow would look great against that wall. Does it grow quickly?

**B:** Yes, that's one of the reasons I chose it, actually. It should reach the top of the wall within a year.

**6 A:** What are you going to plant in this corner?

**B:** Yes, it's very empty. I don't know what to plant. It's really hot in this corner, and the soil gets extremely dry.

**A:** Yes, you're going to need something really hardy.

**B:** How about agave? They're hardy, aren't they?

**A:** Yes, they are. They don't need much water or food, and they can stand really hot temperatures. They can survive just about anything.

**B:** That's what I think I'll have, then.

**18** **Example page 25**

A: Excuse me. I'd like to speak to the Manager, please.

B: I'm the Manager. How can I help you?

A: Well, I'm really unhappy about this carton of milk.

B: And what's the problem, madam?

A: Well. look at it. I bought it here yesterday. See, here's my receipt. And look at the 'use-by' date! It's expired for over a week. Look! The 15th it says, and today's the 23rd. How come you still have old milk in your refrigerators? It's disgusting. I want my money back, and I'm never coming to this supermarket again, I can assure you.

B: Well Madam, I can see why you would be upset. We do always try to …

 **19** **Exercise 17**

**1** Woman: Hey. I heard the good news. That's wonderful. Well done. I'm really happy for you.

Man: Thanks. Yes, I'm really pleased … and relieved that it's all over

Woman: Oh, I never had any doubt that you'd pass. And look, you got a 'distinction'. Well done. You really deserve it.

Man: Thanks. I'm heading over to the student union. I'm going to ring my parents. You coming with me?

**2** Woman: Come on.

Man: I don't want to.

Woman: Oh, come on. I don't want to go by myself. And it's only $25 for students. That's great value. Look, how about this? I'll pay for half of your ticket if you come. Will you come then?

Man: But I'm not that keen on their music.

**3** Woman: It's really four machines in one. It's got a telephone, a fax machine, an answering machine, and a copier. And it's guaranteed for two years.

Man: How much does it cost?

**4** Woman: … The thief is described as being short and stocky with bleached blond hair. Anyone with any information about the robbery should contact the police hotline on 131800. And now for today's highlights in sport, here's Jim. Hi, Jim.

**5** Woman: Hi. I'm interested in the property for sale at Days Road, but I just wanted to check what it says in the advertisement.

Man: Sure. What can I help you with?

Woman: Well, it says the property is being sold with 'vacant possession'? What does that mean?

Man: It simply means that the property will be empty – there won't be any tenants in it – when you buy it.

Woman: Oh, I see.

## Exercise 19

1 I withdrew my application because I did some more thinking about it and decided that I didn't want the job after all.

2 She was hoping to get the job, but it didn't work out. They offered it to another candidate.

3 There are three main types of computer: desktop, laptop, and palmheld.

4 It's a bit cool. Would you mind if I switched off the air-conditioner?

5 There are many advantages to using solar power. It's safer, it's cleaner, and of course it's a lot cheaper in the long run.

6 Good evening. This is a Channel 4 news update. There has been a three-car accident on the South Freeway. Two adults have been killed, and a three-year-old has been taken to General Hospital with severe injuries. The accident occurred at six o'clock this morning. The cause of the accident is unknown, but police have indicated that road conditions after last night's heavy storm may have contributed to the accident.

7 Good afternoon, ladies and gentlemen. Thank you for that warm welcome. My topic today is an important one – exercise programs for the elderly. Most people nowadays would agree that exercise is good for you. But in what ways precisely does it benefit you?

## Exercise 20

Most people assume that ornamental gardens have always existed since the beginning of time. However, this is PAUSE not true, at least as far as Western civilisation is concerned. Although the Chinese were growing plants for aesthetic pleasure at least two thousand PAUSE years ago. In the West, plants were grown for purely practical purposes, such as PAUSE for food, medicine, or for ceremonial use. Well into the fifteenth century gardens were largely limited to crops, orchards and herb gardens. Monasteries in particular had herb gardens where they raised many of the plants which we still use today to PAUSE add flavour to our food. It was only the very wealthy who cultivated anything which was not of practical use. In 16th century English such people were called 'curious gardeners', both because PAUSE they wanted to learn more about plants and because most people regarded them as rather strange.

## Exercise 21

1 A: Excuse me. Can you tell me where the library is?

B: I'm going that way myself. You can walk with me if you like.

A: Thanks.

2 B: Are you new here?

A: Yeh.

B: What are you studying?

A: Economics.

B: Me too. Third year.

A: Really? Third year?

B: Yes. I feel like I've been here forever.

**3** A: How do you find it?

B: I love it. I mean it's hard sometimes, and it's a lot of work, but overall I love it.

**4** A: Do you think we'll get good jobs with our economics degree?

B: I hope so.

A: Me too.

**5** A: I've got to get through this year first, though.

B: Don't worry. you'll be fine.

**6** B: Here's the library.

A: Great. Thanks.

B: Why don't you come inside and I'll show you the economics section.

 **23**   **Exercise 22**

**1** Hi, Lek. How are you? Long time no see.

**2** Excuse me. Does this bus go to the State Library?

**3** Excuse me. Could you press the bell for me, please. I can't quite reach it.

**4** A: I think you should just go to her and explain exactly what happened. Just tell her everything and ask her to forgive you.

B: Really? Do you think I should?

**5** A: I didn't.

B: Yes, you did. You know you did!

A: No, I didn't. I wasn't even there that day!

**6** That's really kind of you. I'd really love to come, but I've got a huge assignment to do this weekend and I'm going to be really busy. I really wish I could come.

**7** It'll be fine, believe me. You'll find it really easy.

**8** It's huge and it's got a really flat screen. And the picture is so clear, it's like being at a cinema.

**9** Why don't you come around on Friday night? We're having a few people over to celebrate Mark's promotion.

**10** I won't take 'no' for an answer.

 **24**   **Examples page 30**

*times:*   a quarter past four, ten to nine, half past twelve

*dates:*   the fifth of March, the twenty-first of November, the thirteenth of February

*numbers:*   three point five, seventeen, seventy, fifth, three quarters, eight and a half million

*letters:*   U-N, U-S-A, S-t-e-v-e-n, I-B-M, c-a-t-e-g-o-r-y, M-a-r-i-a, c-l-i-c-k

**Exercise 23**

**Listen carefully and answer questions 1 to 5.**

A: Kingscliffe Library. Can I help you?

B: Yes. Good morning. I just wanted to ... um ... My library book is due back, but I can't come to the library to return it. I had a bit of an accident and I can't walk at the moment.

A: That's no problem. We can extend it for you. Have you got your library card there?

B: Yes.

A: And what's your membership number? It's on the front, in the bottom, right-hand corner. Can you see it?

B: Oh, yes. It's 0-1-0-3-0 6-9-double-7.

A: Great. Jacqueline Smithies, is that right?

B: Yes, that's right. Well, yes and no. It isn't right strictly speaking. There's always been an error on my card. That's not how you spell my name. My surname.

A: Oh, isn't it? Sorry about that. I'll change it now on the computer while we're here. So, what is it?

B: Well, you've got Smithies, right? S-m-i-t-h-i-e-s.

A: Yes, that's right.

B: Actually it should be Smithers S-m-i-t-h-e-r-s.

A: I see. OK. I've changed it now. But Jacqueline is spelled correctly, is it? J-a-c-q-u-e-l-i-n-e.

B: Yes.

A: OK. We'll post you out a new card with the correct spelling on it.

B: That'd be great.

A: Your postal address is right, isn't it?

B: I think so.

A: 17A Heeley Street, H-double e-l-e-y.

B: Yes, that's it

A: Clapham.

B: Yes. SW11.

A: SW11. Yes, that's right. OK. Well, all that's in order now.

**Listen carefully and answer questions 6 to 10.**

A: Now, what was the book that's due? Oh yes, I see it – yes, it's due tomorrow, the 12th of August.

B: Yes, that's it.

A: Well, I can extend that to the 30th of September. Will that be enough time for you to get it back?

B: Oh, that's plenty of time. Yes, that'll be fine. Thanks.

A: No problem.

B: Listen. While I've got you …

A: Yes?

B: There's a book I'd like to find.

A: Sure. What's the title?

B: Well, that's the problem. I'm not sure. It's about 'hardanger'.

A: Sorry?

B: 'Hardanger' h-a-r-d-a-n-g-e-r. It's a kind of craft, like crocheting, or … sewing, I suppose. I'm not real sure to be honest. It's for my mother. It's her hobby. But I know the author's name.

A: Fine. That's all we need. What's the author's name?

B: Liebke. L-i-e-b-k-e.

A: Do you know when it was published?

B: 1989, I think.

A: Oh, yes. Here it is. 'Hardanger Patterns and Techniques' by Liebke. Is that the one?

B: Yes, I'm sure that's it.

## Listen carefully and answer questions 11 to 15.

A: It's out at the moment, I'm afraid. It's due back on the thirteenth – the thirteenth of August. You could come in and pick it up then if you like. Would you like me to reserve it for you?

B: I could come in at the end of next month. Could you reserve it for then?

A: Done. You can pick it up on the 30th.

B: Thank you. By the way, what times are you open?

A: During the week we open at half past nine and we close at seven o'clock.

B: Seven?

A: Yes. On Saturday and Sunday we close a bit later, at eight thirty.

B: But the same opening time?

A: Yes. The same.

B: Great. Thanks for all your help. What was your name?

A: Axel.

B: Sorry?

A: Axel. A-x-e-l.

B: Thanks a lot, Axel.

A: A pleasure. Bye now.

B: Bye. Thanks.

**26**

## Exercise 24

One of the most widely occurring processes in the world is the production of refined flour from wheat, through a process called 'milling'. There are four main stages in the process. In the first stage, the cleaning stage, the wheat grains, or 'kernels' as they are called, are placed in large bins which contain revolving blades. These remove any dirt or debris, leaving clean kernels for further processing. In the next stage, known as 'conditioning', the kernels are placed under large sprinklers. In this way they are treated with water to 'condition' them – that is, to soften them, to make them soft enough to break in the next stage of the process. The next stage is the actual 'milling' itself. In this milling phase, as we call it, which of course is the key process in the whole operation, the grains are passed between rollers – enormous round rollers. This action splits the kernels and produces the finely ground grains that we know as 'flour'. The flour moves to the 'bleaching' stage where it is placed in large vats and treated with bleaching agents. This makes the flour white. Traditionally, this process was achieved through natural aging. The flour is then mechanically packed in a process known as 'sacking', so called because the flour is placed into large sacks. The flour is then ready for use in baking bread and cake products, and for use in cooking.

 **27**

## Exercise 25

| | |
|---|---|
| **Mr Lee:** | Here, I'll show you what I mean. Have a look at this. (puts something on the table.) Can you all see this? Come a bit closer, you three over there. Yes, that's it. Can you see? |
| **Ben:** | What is it? |
| **Mr Lee:** | Well, what do you think it is? |
| **Ben:** | I don't know. Looks like a thermometer. |
| **Colin:** | No. It's a barometer. |
| **Mr Lee:** | That's right. A barometer. |
| **Ben:** | I thought it was a watch. |
| **Mr Lee:** | Actually it's an aneroid barometer, to be precise. |
| **Ben:** | A what? |
| **Mr Lee:** | Aneroid |
| **Ben:** | Sounds like a robot. |
| **Mr Lee:** | Aneroid a-n-e-r-o-i-d. Don't worry about writing it down – I'll give you a handout on it in a moment. OK. It means non-liquid, that is it doesn't have any liquid, any mercury, which is what is used in the other type of barometer. And of course you know what a barometer is for, don't you? |
| **Colin:** | Measuring … um … moisture in the air, measuring humidity … air pressure. |
| **Mr Lee:** | Yes, that's close enough. This … here I'll show you … this is the critical part inside … it's the vacuum chamber. Can you see it? Some of the air has been taken out of this chamber – that's why it's called a vacuum of course – so that it reacts to air pressure. |

Ben: But how does it work?

Mr Lee: Any changes in air pressure make this chamber contract or expand. This shift is transferred along this series of levers – you see there are two of them, one here connected to another one here.

Ben: Why are they called 'leaders'?

Mr Lee: No, I'm not saying 'leaders', Ben. Levers.

Ben: Oh, sorry. Yes, I see.

Mr Lee: So, the move is transferred along the levers to this chain – just a regular chain, and then the chain wraps around this spindle. 'Spindle', Ben. I don't want you to get it wrong again. Spindle s-p-i-n-d-l-e.

Ben: Got it. Thank you, sir.

Mr Lee: Which, as you can see, in turn drives the needle.

Colin: It moves the needle across the dial.

Mr Lee: Precisely. That's how a barometer measures. And there are three ways to make this measurement – you can use millibars, millimetres, or inches. What does this one use? What's written there on the dial, Ben? Can you see it?

Ben: Where?

Mr Lee: Just near the head of the needle.

Ben: Oh, yes. I can see. 'Inches'.

Colin: What's a millibar?

Mr Lee: Don't worry about that just now. Let's lets take a look at this handout first.

28

*Example*

## Exercise 26

A: How come he arrived so late?

Ben: Because his flight was delayed.

**1** A: Did you hear about that awful car accident?

B: Yes, I heard. Apparently it was all due to driver fatigue.

A: Really?

B: Yes. She'd been driving for ten hours, and fell asleep at the wheel. Sad, isn't it?

**2** A: The 5 per cent fall in the New York stock exchange has led to similar falls in other markets internationally.

**3** A: And of course as a result of all these endless delays we're now 10 days behind schedule.

**4** A: How come her visa application was rejected?

B: She didn't pass the medical test.

**5** A: Environmentalists attribute the recent, record-breaking floods to the erosion which has accompanied the destruction of forests in adjacent foothill areas.

**29**

## Exercise 27

Another English-speaking country in this region is Trinidad and Tobago. The official name of this country is the 'Republic of Trinidad and Tobago', reflecting the fact that the nation comprises two islands, Trinidad and Tobago. Trinidad is the larger of the two islands, with an area of 4,828 square kilometres, whereas Tobago, which is located to the north-east of Trinidad, has a mere 300 square kilometres. As well as in size, the two islands are very different in shape. Trinidad is round in shape while the latter is long and thin. Trinidad is also the higher of the two islands, reaching a maximum elevation of 940 metres, while Tobago reaches a height of only 576 metres. Both islands are densely inhabited, with an estimated 96 per cent of the total population of the country living on Trinidad, and a mere 4 per cent on Tobago. Now united and independent (since 1962), both islands passed through many colonial hands. Trinidad was confirmed as a British possession in 1797, while Tobago was confirmed in British hands in 1814. The two colonies were linked in 1888.

 **30**

## Exercise 28

**1** There are three fares available. The first class fare is $1350, the business class fare is $1030 and the economy fare is $650.

**2** There are two different types of test. One is the so-called Academic Test. This is for candidates seeking to enter university, and it comprises three subjects: English, Computer Literacy, and Mathematics. The other test is the Technical Test. This is for candidates wishing to enter technical college. It is the same as the Academic test, except candidates do not have to take the English component.

**3** Broadly speaking, writing can be divided into two kinds: non-fiction and fiction. In non-fiction writing, for example biographies, textbooks and dictionaries, the content is factual. On the other hand, fiction, such as novels or poems or cartoons, uses imaginary characters and events.

**4** The United Nations employs an enormous group of interpreters, proficient in over one hundred and fifty languages. Without their interpreting services, the UN could not function. There are basically two kinds of interpreting: simultaneous and consecutive. In simultaneous interpreting, the interpreter translates at the same time as the speaker is talking. That's what 'simultaneous' means, of course. The two people overlap in their speaking, with the interpreter lagging just a little behind. In simultaneous interpreting, the speaker does not have to pause. In consecutive interpreting, however, the interpreter translates after the speaker. The speaker pauses, allowing the interpreter to translate what has just been said, before the former then continues. The two people do not overlap.

**5** One of the most fascinating birds in the world is the emu. Emu. E-m-u. This large, flightless bird can reach up to 2 metres in height. There are two varieties of emu: the Western Emu and the Eastern Emu, the names of the varieties reflecting their geographical distribution. There are two features which distinguish the varieties. The first feature is colour, with the Western variety typically having a darker colour. The other feature relates to seasonal change. The Western Emu develops a white 'ruff' (like a white collar around its neck) when it is breeding, whereas the Eastern Emu does not change colour at all during breeding.

**31**

### Exercise 29

**1** There are two versions of the IELTS Reading Test, namely Academic Reading, which of course is the one that most of you here are going to take, and General Training Reading. I won't talk about General Training Reading in detail at the moment, because only two of you are involved.

**2** Languages can be divided into three main types according to their structure, in particular the order of the constituent elements in a sentence. The first (and most common) type contains 'SOV' languages. Here 'S' stands for 'subject', 'O' stands for 'object' and of course 'V' then refers to 'verb'. The second type (and English is an example of this second type) contains 'SVO languages'. The third type contains 'VSO languages'.

**3** English sentences can basically be divided into three types. We'll be looking at the characteristics in detail later. For the time being I'll just give you the names of the three types, namely 'simple sentences', 'compound sentences' and 'complex sentences'. Have you got that? Yes, that's right: (slowly) simple, compound, and complex.

 **32**

### Exercise 30

| | |
|---|---|
| Mrs B: | More coffee anyone? |
| All: | No thanks. |
| Mrs B: | Another piece of cake, Julie? |
| Julie: | No, thanks, Mrs. Blake. It was great. |
| Tom: | Hey, Diane. Have you finished your assignment yet? |
| Diane: | Yes. I handed it in this morning. What about you? |
| Mrs B: | (interrupting): No, of course he hasn't. He's always running late. |
| Tom: | Thank you very much, Mum |
| Mrs B: | Well, it's true, isn't it? |
| Tom: | Yes, I have to admit it. I haven't quite finished it yet. How much is it worth? |
| Diane: | 10 per cent of the final mark, I think. |
| Tom: | All that hard work for just 10 per cent. I hate continuous assessment! The never-ending pressure. |
| Mrs B: | What's 'continuous assessment'? |
| Diane: | Well instead of just having one exam at the end of the year, they give you a mark for each of your assignments throughout the year. And sometimes they give you a mark for how well you participate in tutorials too. |
| Mrs B: | Mmm. Sounds like a good idea to me. I'm sure it makes you study harder throughout the year. I can just imagine how lazy Tom would be if his assignments didn't count. |
| Tom: | Thank you very much, Mum. Of course Diane loves continuous assessment, don't you? |

**Diane:** No, I don't. I hate assignments just as much as you do, but it's still better than just having one formal examination. There's too much stress that way. I get really nervous having to do an exam. This way I've got a better chance of getting a reasonable mark.

**Mrs B:** What about you, Julie? Which method do you prefer?

**Julie:** You know me, Mrs. Blake. I'm a risk-taker. Give me an exam any day. Do or die, I say.

**Tom:** Exactly. And an exam is over in a couple of hours. It's much less painful than all these endless assignments.

**Julie:** And I think it's very fair. Everybody takes the same exam on the same day.

**Diane:** Well, we'd better leave you alone, Tom, so that you can finish your assignment.

**Tom:** Oh, come on. Don't leave. Have another coffee.

 **33**

## Exercise 31

**1** Solar power is our future. It is renewable, it is safe, it is clean. You can't say that about the other major forms of power, such as fossil fuels or nuclear power. No wonder that in 1999 the United Nations described it as, quote, the preferred source of power for the twenty-first century, unquote. Solar power is our only way forward.

**2** Anti-drug television commercials are a waste of time and money, and they should be stopped. The nation-wide survey which our agency conducted throughout April 2001 indicates that the majority of young people do not like the commercials and are not frightened by their message. Also, in the survey interviews, over 60% of young people felt that the commercials were unbalanced, because they did not also target alcohol and tobacco, the drugs used by their parents.

**3** At the moment I'm doing a business degree via the Internet. When you study in distance mode like this, it's great. You feel that you have more control over your study. You can study when you like. You can also manage the pace of your study: you can go more quickly or more slowly. You can pause, repeat, or you can skip things and go ahead. And you can tell that distance study suits me better. I study much harder nowadays than when I went to university. I feel really motivated. I love it.

**4** Marine pollution has reached crisis level around the world, and yet governments appear totally unable or unwilling to acknowledge the extent or significance of the problem. Studies undertaken at our monitoring station at Point Fortitude in the Antarctic indicate a staggering 150 per cent increase in marine pollution since we began taking measurements just three years ago. This rate of increase is frightening. Similar studies conducted by the South African government confirm these fears, and the studies by the Icelandic government, at marine locations the same distance from the pole as in the southern hemisphere studies, show increase rates of over 200 per cent per year.

**5** Critics of the ancient sport of boxing completely miss the point when they call for it to be banned. They claim that it is too dangerous and cite the most recent boxing-related fatality as proof of their claim. I know, and most of you know, that the reality is different. In fact, there are fewer deaths associated with boxing than with just about any other major contact sport, and that includes rugby. In 1999, for example, boxing deaths worldwide were estimated at less than half of rugby deaths. Quite apart from that, boxing is a very positive and much-loved sport. For one thing, it represents an excellent opportunity for young athletes, especially from disadvantaged backgrounds, to excel, to achieve self-esteem, and to achieve a satisfying and lucrative career. And boxing brings great pleasure to millions of fans around the world. Did you know that the most recent world heavyweight championship bout reached a world-wide television audience of over a billion people. What are you going to say to these people? Tell a billion people they are wrong? What are you going to do? Switch off boxing? No, don't be ridiculous. Boxing should most certainly not be banned.

 **32**

## IELTS PRACTICE TEST: LISTENING

You will hear a number of different recordings and you will have to answer questions on what you hear. There will be time for you to read the instructions and questions and you will have a chance to check your work. All the recordings will be played ONCE only.

The test is in four sections. Write your answers in the listening section booklet. At the end of the test you will be given ten minutes to transfer your answers to an answer sheet.

**Now turn to Section 1 on the next page.**

## Section 1

Michael wants to rent an apartment. He is meeting a woman from a real estate office who is going to show him an apartment which is available for rent. Listen to their conversation and answer the questions. First you have some time to look at questions 1 to 6.

### Listen carefully and answer questions 1 to 6.

L: Hello. Are you Mr Lee?

M: Yes. Michael Lee. And you're Ms Addison?

L: Yes. Nice to meet you. Please call me Lisa. Have you been waiting long? It's already 10 past five, I'm sorry. I was a little held up.

M: No, I just arrived.

L: That's good. Well, shall we go inside? The lift's over here.

M: What floor is the apartment on?

L: The third floor. It's apartment 34 on the third floor. Yes, that's it, number 3. Thanks.

M: Is this the only lift in the building?

L: Yes, it is. But as you can see it's quite large and it's very quick. Here we are. After you.

M: Thank you. Hm … the view from here is beautiful.

L: Yes, you can see the beach. And the university's over there. Can you see it?

M: Oh, yes. It's close. I'll be able to walk. That's handy.

L: Will you be living here by yourself?

M: Oh, no. My wife's arriving tomorrow. And we have one child.

L: That's nice. OK Here's the apartment. Number 34. Come in.

M: Thanks.

L: A boy or a girl?

M: Sorry?

L: Do you have a son or a daughter?

M: A daughter. Three years old.

L: Lovely. You see – there are two security locks on the door. Security in this building is excellent – you've got nothing to worry about in that regard.

M: That's good. Hm … but it's very small, isn't it? To be honest, I was hoping for something quite a bit bigger.

L: Yes, I agree it is very small, but it has everything you need – and as you can see it's beautifully furnished.

M: So the furniture comes with it – at the price advertised in the paper?

L: Yes, everything you see is included. It's really good value.

M: Does that include electricity and water and gas and things like that?

L: Water's included, but not electricity and gas – they're your responsibility.

M: OK. Now … there are two bedrooms, right?

L: Yes. One over there next to the kitchen and the main bedroom is right here. Yes, go on in.

M: Hm … it's really quite small.

L: True, but look at the storage. Look at the wardrobes, and the set of shelves over on that wall. There's plenty of storage. You've even got these drawers under the bed.

M: There's not enough storage, actually.

L: Not enough?

M: Well, we have a huge amount of books and clothes and things.

L: And again you have a lovely view from here, this time facing north.

M: Yes. Could I see the kitchen?

L: Yes. Just over here.


M and L continue looking at the apartment. First look at questions 7 to 10.

## Now listen and answer questions 7 to 10. Write no more than three words for each answer.

M: Yes. Now what else? Oh, yes, the bathroom.

L: I think you'll like the bathroom. It's right here next to the kitchen.

M: Hm, very nice. Very clean.

L: Yes. It's excellent, isn't it?

M: What about the laundry?

L: There's a shared laundry – one on each floor, so that means there's just three apartments sharing, which is fine. And it has an excellent washing machine. Shall we go and have a look?

M: OK.

L: So, what do you think overall?

M: Well, it's quite nice. Can I bring my wife tomorrow to have a look?

L: Yes, of course, but I'm afraid I won't be available tomorrow. My colleague could show you through, though, probably around this time, five o'clock. Would that suit you?

M: That's fine. Actually, I'd prefer a bit later if possible.

L: Well, shall we make it six? I'm sure he could make that time, if you prefer.

M: How about half past five?

L: OK. Let's agree on that, then. I'm sure that'll be fine for him. But I wonder if you'd mind giving him a call tomorrow yourself, just to confirm the appointment. I'll give you his mobile phone number.

M: Yes, what is it?

L: It's 0418 327704.

M: 0418 327704. Great. Oh, and what's your colleague's name?

L: His name's Eric Bana. E-R-I-C. No, sorry. It's E-R-I-C. Yes, that's it. And then Bana. B-A-N-A.

M: B-A-N-A. Thanks. I'll phone him tomorrow.

L: That'll be fine. Ah, here we are. The laundry.

**That is the end of section 1. You now have half a minute to check your answers.**

**Now turn to section 2 on the next page.**

## Section 2

You are going to hear Alison giving a briefing to new staff. In the first part of the briefing, she is explaining the procedures for staff entering the building. First look at questions 11 to 14.

**As you listen to the first part of the briefing, answer questions 11 to 15. Write no more than three words for each answer.**

Good morning, ladies and gentlemen. My name is Alison Subroto, and my position here at SU is Head of Security. I'd like to have your attention for an important demonstration. Thank you. The information I'm about to give you may not be the most exciting information you'll hear today, but it's probably the most important.

Let's start with the procedures for staff entering the building. As you would probably already be aware, this building contains a laboratory, and is therefore a high-security facility. This door is the only entrance to the interior of the building. There is only one way through that door, and that is to use your staff card, the card which is issued to every new member of staff. Staff are given a personal identification number or PIN (Personal Identification Number) which they must memorise. Please make sure that you don't write this number on the card itself. If you forget your number, you can speak to the security officer, and he or she will contact the Personnel Section.

OK. Now let's check how it is used. Hold it with the top of the card facing the door, like this. Can you all see? Good. Now, pass it through quickly, in one movement. Sometimes, if you swipe it too slowly, it won't work. So swipe it through smoothly and quickly, and immediately you should hear a click – you hear that? you hear that click? Here, I'll do it again. It's very straightforward. OK, then as soon as you hear that click, you need to enter your PIN. There is a key pad here with all the numbers. If the machine accepts your number, then this light will immediately flash green and the door will open. OK, that's pretty well the main procedures for staff coming into the laboratory.

**In the second part of the briefing, Alison goes on to explain the procedures for visitors. First look at questions 16 to 18.**

As you listen, complete the table showing the information which visitors must provide. Write no more than three words for each answer.

Now let's check the procedures for visitors. When visitors arrive at reception, they must nominate a contact person on the laboratory staff. The security officer at reception will ask them to telephone the staff member whom they are visiting on this telephone – there's a directory of extension numbers here on the reception desk. Then, if you are the staff member contacted, you must come to reception. If you are not available, the visitor will not be admitted. OK. Now, when you come down and join your visitor at reception, they must then fill out this register. I've put the register up here on the projector so that you can all see. Please make sure – I can't stress this too strongly – please make sure that your visitor fills in all the details you can see here, and I mean all: 'Name', 'Organisation' (their company, department, etc), their 'Purpose of visit', naturally enough – are they coming here for a meeting for example – 'Staff contact' (the name of the person they are visiting), 'Date' (the date of the visit of course), and 'Time in' (of course, the time the visit begins). Don't fill in the 'time out' column yet of course – that's for when the visitor leaves.

Before the briefing continues, look at questions 19 to 20.

## As you listen, answer questions 19 to 20.

After the visitors' register is completed, the security officer will then issue the visitor with a visitor's card, like this one here. As you can see, visitors' cards are a very different colour from staff cards, and are immediately recognisable as such. Then you can accompany the visitor through the security door, opening it of course with your staff card. The visitor's card will not open the door. Once inside the laboratory, visitors must wear the visitor's card where it is easily visible throughout their visit. Please make sure that your visitors are aware of the security importance of complying with these regulations. When the visit is finished, and they return to the lobby, the security officer will ask them to return their visitor's card and to complete 'time out' in the register, here – that is the time they are leaving. Here in the last column of the visitors' register. I realise that all of these regulations and procedures may seem a little time-consuming and tedious, but it's essential that you conform with them. That's about it. Thanks very much for your attention. Are there any questions?

**That is the end of section 2. You now have half a minute to check your answers.**

**Now turn to section 3 on the next page.**

## Section 3

In this section you are going to listen to a conversation between three university students, Martin, Jack, and Mary. Martin and Jack are first-year university students, studying law. They are talking to Mary about the Law Students Association. First look at questions 21 to 27.

**Now listen to their conversation and answer the questions. Write no more than three words for each answer.**

| | |
|---|---|
| Martin: | This is it, Jack. The Law Students Association. |
| Jack: | Right. Hi. |
| Mary: | Hi. |
| Jack: | I'm Jack … and this is Martin. |
| Martin: | Hi. This is the Law Students Association, right? |
| Mary: | Yes, that's right. My name's Mary. I'm the President of the Association. Are you interested in joining? |
| Martin: | Maybe. What year are you in? |
| Mary: | Fourth year. |
| Jack: | We're both in first year. |
| Martin: | I'm not sure if we'll survive even into second year. |
| Mary: | I'm sure you'll make it fine. It does seem a bit daunting at the beginning, but it gets easier. Trust me. |
| Jack: | That's hard to imagine. |
| Martin: | So, do you have to pay to join the Law Students Association? |
| Mary: | Well, there's an annual membership fee of 10 pounds, or you can get five-year membership for 35 pounds. |
| Jack: | And what do you get for that? |
| Mary: | Well, we put out two newsletters a year and of course you get those for free, and you get discount on any social events that we organise. |
| Jack: | Like what? |
| Mary: | Well, we have the Law Ball every year. |
| Jack: | The what? |
| Martin: | The Law Ball! You must have heard of it. It's the biggest dance of the year! They say it's terrific. |
| Mary: | It sure is. And instead of paying 25 pounds which is what we charge non-members, you only have to pay 5 pounds, which is really good value considering all the food and drink and entertainment. |
| Jack: | Mm, well I'm not much of a dancer. In fact, I don't dance at all, I'm afraid. What else is there? |
| Mary: | Well, we have guest speakers. You know, prominent people – judges, barristers, and so on – talking about topics. There's a Guest Seminar |

the first Tuesday of every month. The first one's tomorrow, actually. Five o'clock.

Jack: Mmm. That sounds great. I'd love to hear about their experience. But my timetable is so full already. I don't think I have enough time to go to guest seminars, even if they're only once a month. Any other activities?

Mary: Well, we offer some free peer coaching.

Martin: Peer coaching? What's that? Sounds like you're mixing study and sport.

Jack: Don't be silly, Martin. It's when other students help you, coach you, if you're having problems with your study.

Mary: That's right. Usually we get the senior students – third or fourth years – to do it.

Martin: Great. I think that could be very useful for me. I reckon I'm going to need a lot of help to get through this first year. And it's great that it's free.

Mary, Jack and Martin continue talking about the Association. First read questions 28 and 29.

**Now answer questions 28 and 29. Write no more than three words for each answer.**

Jack: What else does the Association get involved in?

Mary: Well, we arrange second-hand book sales. Law books, of course. They're a lot cheaper, being second-hand.

Jack: Yes, I saw them being sold over near the library.

Mary: Yes, that's it. In front of the library.

Jack: I wish I'd known about it earlier. I've just paid a fortune for all my law textbooks. All brand new.

Mary: Well, next year you can sell some of those books second-hand and get some of your money back.

Jack: Yes, I suppose so. Well that makes me feel a bit better.

Martin: Well, I think you've got two new members.

Mary: Terrific.

Jack: Ah, I think I might wait a bit. I'm a bit short of money at the moment.

Martin: Do you want me to lend you some, Jack?

Jack: No, thanks.

Martin. OK, if you're sure. (To Mary) Can I pay and sign up now?

Mary: Just put your details here on this form. Sorry, what was your name again?

Martin: Martin.

**That is the end of section 3. You now have half a minute to check your answers.**

**Now turn to section 4 on the next page.**

## Section 4

You will listen to an extract from a university lecture about culture shock. First you have some time to look at questions 31 to 38.

**As you listen to the first part of the lecture, answer questions 31 to 36. Write no more than three words for each answer.**

I'd like to focus on a critical issue in culture – namely 'culture shock'. You may have heard the term before. Have you? Yes, I can see some of you nodding. Perhaps you've even experienced it yourself – yes, again I can see some of you nodding, so obviously you have experienced it. Maybe you experienced it without even knowing the term and not really understanding what you were going through. So what is this term 'culture shock'? I want to look at its meaning, its causes, and its manifestations. Time permitting, we'll move on to possible responses. OK?

But first a word about your assignments. What I'm covering today will be useful in your second assignment. OK? Your second assignment, which, just to remind you, should be well under way by now. I'm expecting it from you no later than the 28th, remember.

OK. What is culture shock? 'The result of the removal of the familiar'. That's how Brick puts it – and I think it's a pretty good definition. The things that are familiar to us, we tend to take for granted and tend not to be aware of, and of course that's the whole point behind culture shock, because suddenly we do become aware that things are not proceeding as we are used to. Take away the familiar, and suddenly you're experiencing culture shock.

And then of course there are those things that are even harder to see at first – things like values – do you remember the research studies on value systems I mentioned last week? Well, to show what we mean by 'different values' we can take a look at essays. That's an example that should be close to home for all of you. What is a good essay? There's certainly no universal agreement about that. So you might find that you go to another country for further study, like many of you here today, and suddenly your essays, which were always regarded as very well written in your home country, are now criticised for being badly organised or containing irrelevant material. Yes, I can see that's struck a chord with some of you.

When values conflict, the result can be culture shock. Values are often called the iceberg of intercultural communication. Why 'iceberg'? Well, as you probably know, an iceberg is invisible, or at least the vast majority of it is. So too are our values – they're invisible. They underlie everything in our society, determining what's right, what's appropriate, what's good. Like, what constitutes a good lecturer? Well, maybe we'd better not get into that one.

So, culture as iceberg. And, believe me, just as the ships looking out for icebergs usually don't hit them, so too people who are ready, people who expect that they will experience some culture shock when they move to another environment, they're the very ones who'll probably experience less shock than others. People who think they're not going to have a problem with culture shock usually end up having far more shock. Ironic, but true, at least as far as the research shows.

In the next part of the lecture the speaker continues to examine culture shock.

First look at questions 37 and 38.

**Now answer questions 37 to 38. Circle two letters in each answer.**

OK, so how does culture shock manifest itself? Do people go around dazed and pale, like say after they've been in a car accident? Is it that kind of shock? Well, in a way, yes, it is, even if people don't actually turn pale. In fact, the symptoms of culture shock are rather similar to the symptoms of severe stress that you might get from a trauma in your life – say losing your job, or having your house burn down, or being seriously ill, and so on. We would all recognise that these events trigger great stress, but we tend to forget the fact that culture shock can have a similar impact. Commonly, the person experiencing culture shock feels frustrated, helpless and unhappy, each of which of course has a physical expression – such as fatigue, headaches, weight loss (or gain, with some people) and anxiety, and so on. Indeed, these symptoms can be very severe, so much so that one would have to say that culture shock constitutes a serious risk to physical and mental health. Yes. Culture shock is very dangerous.

So, how do people react in these situations? Often, in trying to make sense of what is happening to them, people will blame the society – you know, things like 'the people here are not friendly', 'the people here are not polite', 'the teachers here don't know how to teach', and so on. What they're saying in effect of course is 'they're not following my rules' but they don't see it this way. So they attribute their difficulties to the society, not to their situation as new entrants into that society.

Next week we'll have a look at how people can go about reducing the effects of culture shock. I want you to come to next week's lecture well prepared, so during the week please read Chapter 1 of Brick, and answer the questions at the end of the chapter, so that you'll be ready to think about some of the issues we'll be discussing. But first let's look at this. We've still got a few minutes. Could you turn the lights off, please.

In the final part of the lecture the speaker describes the typical pattern of culture shock. First look at questions 39 and 40.

**Listen carefully and answer questions 39 and 40. Write no more than three words for each answer.**

Thanks. Can everyone see the projector? Great. OK. Here is the typical pattern for culture shock. At the beginning, on entering the new environment, the mood is often upbeat, very high. The person finds the new environment interesting, intriguing, and so on, but then attitudes can plunge as the problems start happening, as culture shock registers, then a gradual improvement, with the mood coming up, as the person learns to understand and cope with the environment, and then it reaches a stable ongoing pattern, like a plateau. In this stage, culture shock is largely resolved, for better or worse. The easy way to remember this pattern is this – there are three phases in the curve: 'honeymoon' (everything is great), 'divorce' (I hate this, I want to get out of here), and 'marriage' (OK, I guess we can live together) – which of course is rather different from the usual pattern.

I can see some of you smiling, but culture shock really can be as severe as divorce, and living in a different cultural environment really is like a marriage, when you think about it. Just like marriage, succeeding in a different cultural environment takes some hard work and effort. You can't just sit back and take it easy, do nothing. And like marriage, living in a different culture has its ups and downs. There are good times and bad. Sometimes there are times when you really don't understand each other, where there's a communication breakdown. But slowly you get to know each other's quirks and strengths and weaknesses, and that's what you need to do with culture too – learn more. And of course slowly learn to adjust to each other. I'm not saying … some people think you have to change yourself inside when you live in a different cultural environment. That's not the way I see it, though, and I think the research backs me up. You don't have to change yourself, although you do ultimately need to make some adjustments. Some adjustments in your behaviour at least, if not your 'inside', your 'spirit', your 'self'. Anyway, I see our time is up, so I'll leave it there. Now next week, as I said, we'll …

**That is the end of section 4. You now have half a minute to check your answers.**

**That is the end of the Practice IELTS Listening Test.**

**At the end of the real IELTS Listening Test you will have ten minutes to transfer your answers to the Listening Answer Sheet.**

**UNIT 2: SPEAKING**
**Exercise 3**

| | |
|---|---|
| Examiner: | Yes, that's fine. Thank you. Let's talk about your study or work. Are you currently studying or do you work? |
| Candidate: | I am a student, yes, studying. |
| Examiner: | And why did you choose this particular course? |
| Candidate: | You mean, the course in the university? |
| Examiner: | Mm. |
| Candidate: | Yeah, because, actually it's more easy to find a job becau ... if you are an accountant. Yeah, I'm studying accounting. |
| Examiner: | Mm. And what are the most challenging or difficult things about your course of study? |
| Candidate: | Yeah. I think the most difficult thing is there are a lot of difference in different company. I mean, the situation is quite different, and use which kind of method to data the, the, to data the figures or something else, I mean, as well use different methods. It is a big challenge because different situation in different situation you need to use different methods so maybe this method is especially suitable for that company. Yet you need a lot of experience, yeah. |
| Examiner: | Mm. And what do you think you'll do when your course finishes? |
| Candidate: | I think I will find a job in Australia and to earn more, ah, experience, because become accountant experience is much more important than the degree. |
| Examiner: | Mm. Now let's move on to talk about learning languages. |
| Candidate: | Mm. |
| Examiner: | Would you say you are good at speaking other languages? |
| Candidate: | Um, I think that's okay if you keep on practising and practising, will be better. |
| Examiner: | Mm. Why do you think some people are better at learning languages than other people? |
| Candidate: | I think that there talent. Yes, some people they are born to be good at learning some languages. I think that's it. |
| Examiner: | And do you think some second languages are easier to learn than other second languages? |
| Candidate: | Mm, I don't think so but I have no experience, I just, that's just my opinion. |
| Examiner: | Okay. What do you think is the most effective way to learn a language? |
| Candidate: | Effective? I think, um, more listening, um, more practice. I think you can, um, use a tape there, for example, when you listen to |

English and you follow them sentence by sentence and speak much quickly and quickly each time. Then you keep going every day, I think, is most effective.

Examiner: Let's talk a little about your country. Have you travelled around it much?

Candidate: Um, I think just a small part of our country because China is a large country. And I just travel about some big cities.

Examiner: What's the most popular region in your country for overseas tourists?

Candidate: Region? Um, I'm sorry, I know but I don't know how to describe in English. I don't know that, the name of that region.

Examiner: Is there a particular city that's um, that's popular for tourists?

Candidate: Oh yes, yeah. The big cities, for example, the Beijing, Shanghai, Guangzhou, Sindran and Hong Kong nowadays.

### 2   Exercise 5

Examiner: Can you start speaking now, please.

Candidate: Yes. Ah, the thing I wo … own that's most important from me, it's my car, it's in Brazil. Um, my father gave me this four years ago and it is the most important thing because I, I have a few problems travelling by bus or train. Because of the movement I have a problem here in my labyrinth so I feel a little bit sick for the whole trip. And it's the best thing, because I can … not only because of this disease, if I can call like this, but it's the moment I can stay alone, listen to my music in peace without a lot of people bother me. Not exactly bother me but I feel more comfortable because I can think of my day, I can think of everything happen and listen to my music, but it's always more comfortable and, than travelling by train or bus.

### 3   Exercise 9

*Speaker One*

Examiner: Ah hah. Okay, we've been talking about places where people live. I'd like now to discuss one or two general questions relating to this topic. First, let's consider the recent development of a city you know well. To what extent was this development a result of planning?

Candidate: Mm. I'm not so sure. Are you asking me about a city planning?

Examiner: Yes, that's right.

Candidate: So ah, you mean that what do I think about …

Examiner: Yes, to what extent was the development of this city the result of planning?

Candidate: Mm. I think ah, if the city have got a very good planning, the way people live will be more organised, so I think that, um, planning, city planning is important for people who live in.

**Examiner:** Mm. And was um, the city that you know well, was, was um, the development of this city a result of planning?

**Candidate:** Um, I'm not so sure about this because, um, I haven't been to many places but I can give you an example in Australia because I got like a, a direct experience here. I think that in Sydney, especially in the, in the … um, how can I say, the, the area nearby the city are quite well organised. For example, in, in, North Ryde, Epping, there are, there are um, parks. So people can enjoy their free time over there.

**Examiner:** Ah hah.

**Candidate:** Yeah, but for in Thailand, we haven't got that much space, especially in the, in the central part of Bangkok.

**Examiner:** Ah hah. We've seen the development of 'gated communities' um, quite a lot recently. Those are communities that are maintained and guarded by private companies, and they're restricted um, to non-residents. Why do you think people may choose to live in these kind of communities?

**Candidate:** Ah, ah, it's … it's very challenging question but I'm not so sure the word that, that you ask me. Ah, the 'gated community', is that mean the um, private property?

**Examiner:** Yes, that's right, guarded by private companies. And only residents are allowed in, normally.

**Candidate:** Ah hah, yes. Um, you ask me whether this is good for people to live there or what?

**Examiner:** Why do you think people choose to live in these kind of communities?

**Candidate:** I think that it will be more safe for people, ah, to live over there because it had been guarded perfectly, I think. So people who would like to be secured, they prefer to live there but I think for that, that, that place you've got to pay a lot in order to live there.

*Speaker Two*

**Examiner:** Okay. We've been talking about places where people live. I'd like now to discuss one or two general questions related to this topic. Let's firstly consider the recent development of a city that you know well. To what extent was this development a result of planning?

**Candidate:** Planning?

**Examiner:** Mm.

**Candidate:** You mean, the city plan, planning of city?

**Examiner:** That's right.

**Candidate:** Okay. I think the big city, you know, there are a lot of big cities in, nowadays, and it developed hod … very quickly and become larger and larger. It cost some programmes. I mean, it's, it have some advantages and some disadvantages so I think planning is very important to, to the city development.

**Examiner:** Mm. Um, what about um, transport. We'll talk about transport now within cities. Um, what are the different ways that people move around um, a city that you know well. Beijing, for example, or where you come from?

**Candidate:** I think there are, there are several method can be used for transportation. First, first is a bus, yeah, when a lot of people take, take buses to move in the city. And second, secondly, is a subway, in some big cities in China like Beijing has a subway as a very good choice for transportation. And the second um, maybe private car and, and other like motor, motorcycle, motorbike and this. But, you know, in China a very, a lot of people take, ride bicycles as transportation.

**Examiner:** Mm. Ah. And do you think the influence of a good system, a good public transportation system – how do you think that influences the people's lives who live there?

**Candidate:** The 'influence' – can you explain what is this?

**Examiner:** Yes, how does it affect the way people live, if you have a good transport system? How does that make a difference to how people live?

**Candidate:** Ah yes. I think transportation, transport in modern cities is very important and in, in most of China cities like Beijing, Guangzhou, people very care about the transport. They always choose the place in like a building, likes their ah, work area and living apartment has, which has, which have good transportation service.

## Exercise 10

*Speaker One*

**Examiner:** Ah, let's first consider the design of modern cities. Can you describe the recent development of a city that you know well?

**Candidate:** Recent development? Let me see. Okay. Ah, when I, when I visit United States it was very modern, modern city, and ah, and was why, you know, in Japan it's very, the city is very messy. So the airport is always entrance for the foreigners but ah, in Japan the access to the airport is very hard, ah, unconvenient.

**Examiner:** Ah hah.

**Candidate:** But in United States, ah, it different. So ah …

**Examiner:** So to what extent do you think the development of these two cities was a result of planning? How would you compare them?

**Candidate:** Yes, maybe, ah. Mm, United States is not so old country and it was, the city has been developed, ah, for, for within one hundred years or so. Or something.

**Examiner:** Mm. Yeah. Okay.

| Candidate: | And it was planned to, to be comfortable for the people. |
|---|---|
| Examiner: | Okay, yeah. How important is planning in shaping development in cities? |
| Candidate: | Cities? Mm, maybe like Australia, ah, there are m …, if there are many natures, trees, it be a very comfortable for the people who are living. And, mm, also we need big street, yeah, and, ah, that, ah, good access to the downtown area. |
| Examiner: | Okay. What do you, what do you think large cities will be like in the future? Will they be more planned or less planned? |
| Candidate: | Less planned? |
| Examiner: | Yeah. Will there be more planning or less planning in cities in the future? |
| Candidate: | Ah, it's … maybe more planning is necessary for the future cities. Mm, I don't know how to, how should, how they should plan to the city but, mm, planning is always necessary. |
| Examiner: | Okay. Um, now, onto another topic here. Um, transport within cities. Think of a city that you know well and what are some of the different ways peoples move, people move about in this city? |
| Candidate: | Yeah, so, in my home country many people use train or buses. Not the same, we may use train to commute or to go somewhere else. And to use car is, ah, limited, you know. We have less car park and to have own car is very, ah, costly. |
| Examiner: | So how many families have cars? |
| Candidate: | Maybe, ah, most of, most families have cars but they can't, they can't use as they want because very, lot, lot of, you know, amusement facility has very expensive car park also. |
| Examiner: | Mm. Okay. In what day, way does a good system of public transportation affect the quality of life for city dwellers? |
| Candidate: | Yeah. Public. Mm, public transportation? For the public buses I sometimes very confused to, how to use the buses and which bus is going which, ah, which place, you know. And so, how to pay a fee is different from the each cities. It's very confusing. |
| Examiner: | Okay. All right. How do you think people will travel round cities in the next century? |
| Candidate: | Next century, yes. Ah, yes, maybe, ah, to go abroad is very common, I think, to become common. And ah, so, the air fee, airplane fees will be, will be very cheap. And so that every, everyone can go overseas. Yeah. |
| *Speaker Two* Examiner: | Okay. Okay. We've been talking about places where people live. I'd like now to discuss one or two general questions relating to this topic. |
| Candidate: | Yes. |

| Examiner: | Firstly, ah, let's consider the recent development of a city you know well. To what extent was this development a result of planning? |
|---|---|
| Candidate: | Ah, okay. This one is a little bit difficult. I will try, if I can put it this way. The city I know, I would like to use the example of um, the capital city that I'm coming from, Taipei. |
| Examiner: | Mm. |
| Candidate: | The government has ah, planning to build the city of Taipei as one of the international city. So the government have been putting quite a lot of the public transportation, for example. Um, so, and also knocking down some old buildings and they put quite a lot of parks. And ah, some very big shopping centres, for example, as well. |
| Examiner: | And do you think large cities will become more or less planned in the future? |
| Candidate: | I think they will become more planned and actually that is one of the needs that people actually want, because I think more and more people want to doing their business in their commercial area. And when they want to relax, when they want to enjoy their family life, they don't want to hear some, like, a commercial, you know, like announcement all the time, the people are doing business or they will put very loud music. I think they would just like enjoy their own family life in the com … residential area. |
| Examiner: | Mm. We've seen the development of a lot of communities called 'gated communities' recently, which are guarded by private companies and you um, you don … it restricts the entry to non-residents so only residents can go in. Why do you think people choose to live in these kind of communities? |
| Candidate: | Um, gated community. Ah, just let me check if I got the idea right. Does that mean the people live in the area, then there's a main entrance that everyone they, they want to go in and leave, they have to go through that main gate? |
| Examiner: | That's right, yes. |
| Candidate: | All right. Um, I think security probably the major reason, ah, so if people who choose to live in the gated community, they probly, probably – oh, sorry, I have the problem with that word. They perhaps, the reason for them to choose is for the concern of security, as I just say earlier. Ah, they were think that um, some people, if they want to pass or go into the community, they would have to pass some, some guard or things like that. |

**🎤 5**

*Speaker One*

## Exercise 13

| Candidate: | I like, I like living there because, um, because um, the culture is ah, similar, similar to my culture. Um, the language is the same language. Um, we are all, we all say, ah, Cantonese. And it's, and |
|---|---|

we, and, ah, and Hong Kong is when, is, is near, um, is near my home town Guangzhou. So um, if I live there, if I live there, ah, I think, ah, it will be very convenience. And I, I like, I like living in Hong Kong because um, everything is very convenience and I, I can, I can eat, I can eat cheaply and I can ah, bought many things because Hong Kong is a shopping haven.

*Speaker Two*

**Examiner:** Okay. Remember you have one to two minutes for this. I'll stop you when the time is up. Can you start speaking now, please.

**Candidate:** Yes. Mm, I think my recent unit is a very good place for living and I, when I arrived Australian I, I rent this unit from my agent, agent, as you say. Yeah, it's apartment on the floor sec … on the second floor and um, it is on the corner of the Fontenoy Road and the Lane Cove Road. Ah, it's bed, it has two bedroom and a laundry and a kitchen and a bathroom. Mm, I like it because I think, firstly, I can, I live here very comfortable and secondly, I think the view is very good. You know, in front of, in front of my unit it's a park. And the bus stop just at the corner so I can take buses very convinced. And secondly, and ah, I think this and the rent is very cheap. So it save me a lot of money. I think another thing is I, my friend, my flatmate is very friend and kind, real kind. It's very easy to get along with her so I'm like my unit very much and I, I enjoy the living very much.

## Examples pages 70–71

**6**

**Examiner:** In what day, way does a good system of public transportation affect the quality of life for city dwellers?

**Candidate:** Yeah. Public. Mm, public transportation? For the public buses I sometimes very confused to, how to use the buses and which bus is going which, ah, which place, you know. And so, how to pay a fee is different from the each cities. It's very confusing.

**7**

**Examiner:** Okay. Why do you think some people are better at learning languages than other people?

**Candidate:** Um, maybe they're very clever. They're clever, than a lot of people and, um, and maybe they work hard.

**8**

**Examiner:** Why do you think some people are better at learning languages than other people?

**Candidate:** Ah, I think that some people do better in some languages because if the languages that they are studying has got, like, the same um, language structure, this will be much more easier for them to, to, um, handle with the language.

**9**

## Exercise 19

*Speaker One*

**Examiner:** How important is planning in guiding the development in a city?

**Candidate:** In a city, um, I think, ah, um, besides the transportation and it is very important, ah, besides the transportation and include the policy of the government, um, ah, it, um. I think the government should spend, should pay more attention to, ah, its ta … to the education. Mm, and let the people know how to be a good person and live in their modern city. Yeah, I think, I think, ah, the spirit is very important.

*Speaker Two*

**Examiner:** Ah hah. Why do you think some people are better at learning languages than other people?

**Candidate:** Um, possibly because they're, the needs. I mean, people, some people, they are more interested in other cultures – then they had the motivation to learn the other languages. Then possibly that's the reason they are a better speakers than the others.

🎤 **10**

## Example page 75

**Examiner:** Well, what's the most popular region in your country for an overseas tourist if I was to come and visit?

**Candidate:** I think in my country most people have no relig … yeah?

🎤 **11**

## Exercise 23

*Speaker One*

**Examiner:** Okay. Remember you have one to two minutes for this. I'll stop you when the time is up. Can you start speaking now, please.

**Candidate:** Yes. Ah, the place that I, ah, I have enjoyed living is, um, Kyoto City. I grew up and, ah, I, so, ah. I went to the university in Kyoto and it was very fine. Ah, Kyoto is a very popular city for foreigners but I think Kyoto is a, has another as … aspect, so it is a city of students. Kyoto has many school, high school and especially universities, so I was attending one of these universities. And Kyoto has a lot of, um, entertaining place and a, and the cheap restaurants, as well as the very traditional temples or shrines. So I didn't go any, any temples or shrines though, but I enjoyed living, to living, to live Kyoto. So, um …

*Speaker Two*

**Examiner:** I'll stop you when the time is up. Can you start speaking now, please.

**Candidate:** Um, ah, this kind of place that you have enjoy(n)ing living. I, um, I think, ah, this place is Sumjin, this, ah, is a city in China. This, Sumjin is very close to Hong Kong and, um, this city is a first year, economic open market, open economic marketer, in China. Um, I, I have been Sumjin nine years. I work there, I work to this pl … in Sumjin, at Sumjin, um, nine years. So ah, this is the first time I left my parents, go out, went out and live alone, just myself. So first day I felt it's very freedom, no parents, take, take after me, so it's very freedom and, um, I were, I, when I went to Sumjin as soon as I got a job. So I, think I'm very lucky in Sumjin. This is a and um, family, um. The city is very beautiful and, ah, the people's living style, standard is not very high, just a litt ... just in middle. Um, and I have a lot of friend, a lot of friend in this city. So I very like living this place.

## 🎤12 Examples page 79

Candidate: Um, I think security probably the major reason. Ah, so if people who choose to live in the gated community, they plobably, plobably (oh, sorry, I have the problem with that word). They perhaps, the reason for them to choose is for the concern of security, as I just say earlier.

## 🎤13

Examiner: Mm. What do you think is the most effective way to learn a language?

Candidate: To practise, to use it, to – yep, just to use it, um, with the people from that language, from that culture. I think that's the best way.

## 🎤14 Exercise 24

Candidate: I believe TV news more than Internet.

Examiner: Why?

Candidate: Because I think on television is, on air to everybody and every day but Internet is, is not so far – govern ... I don't know how to say.

## 🎤15 Exercise 27

*Speaker One*

Examiner: Okay. Remember you have one to two minutes for this. I'll stop you when the time is up. Can you start speaking now, please.

Candidate: Yes, um. Where is the place that I have enjoyed living? Um, there are many places that I have been visited and Sukhothai Province is one of the place that I have um, enjoy living in over there. Ah, there are many reasons why I like to live there. First, ah, first reasons it is its environment and its surroundings. Second reason is people over there are really nice and friendly. Thirdly, Sukhothai Province is not located far from Bangkok where I live. Is what ... it is about five hundred kilometres from Bangkok and is it located ah, northern part of Thailand. Ah, Sukhothai Province, um, was the first um, dynasty, ah, of Thailand. So over there, there are many, many historical sites so that Sukhothai is a very popular place for foreigner. Secondly, ah, I liked Sukhothai because um, I met many friendly people over there. For example, like five years I went to Sukhothai to do some my research, to correct the data, with religious in, in one village at Sukhothai. Over that period of time I had a lot of good experience with the, with people over there.

*Speaker Two*

Candidate: Yes. Um, the place that I have enjoyed living is called Armidale. It's um, in Australia. It is actually about eight hours away from Sydney and um, it's a very small town. Um, the reason I like Armidale is because they got ... Armidale got a different face, let me put it in this way, in every season. Like, in spring we can see the different types of flowers along the street and summer is very, very green. And it's not that hot, as well. It's not as hot as Sydney. And my favourite season is in the autumn because of the trees. And I heard from my friends that those trees are originally from England. And that's why the university there, called the University of New England, I think. And um, the winter – it's quite cold, I would say, compared with my country. Um, but snow. Actually, I haven't seen snow there yet.

Also, it's a very conven … although there is no many um, shopping centres there but I would say it's very convenient for me if I want to do any, any kind of shopping there. Also, what else, mm?

## 🎤 16 Exercise 33

*Speaker One*

Yes. Ah, the thing I wo … own that's most important for me, it's my car, it's in Brazil. Um, my father gave me this four years ago and it is the most important thing because I, I have a few problems travelling by bus or train, because of the movement I have a problem here in my labyrinth so I feel a little bit sick for the whole trip. And it's the best thing, because I can … not only because of this disease, if I can call like this, but it's the moment I can stay alone, listen to my music in peace without a lot of people bother me. Not exactly bother me but I feel more comfortable because I can think of my day, I can think of everything happen and listen to my music, but it's always more comfortable and, than travelling by train or bus. But when someone is with me, it's okay also because the conversation, it's, it's easy to con …, to talk in a quiet environment than in bus or train. So I really, really, really love my car because I don't feel sick, I can organise myself with my time. Ah, just … I just have to think about the traffic, I don't have to think about the timetable of the train, the timetable of the bus. I just organise what time I need to take my car and do whatever I want. I don't depend on anyone when I want to go out. I can go what time I want to go and come back the time I want to go, to come back.

*Speaker Two*

Yeah, it's apartment on the floor sec … on the second floor and um, it is on the corner of the Fontenoy Road and the Lane Cove Road. Ah, it's bed, it has two bedroom and a laundry and a kitchen and a bathroom. Mm, I like it because I think, firstly, I can, I live here very comfortable and secondly, I think the view is very good. You know, in front of, in front of my unit it's a park. And the bus stop just at the corner so I can take buses very convinced. And secondly, and ah, I think this and the rent is very cheap. So it save me a lot of money. I think another thing is I, my friend, my flatmate is very friend and kind, very kind. It's very easy to get along with her so I'm like my unit very much and I, I enjoy the living very much.

## 🎤 17 Exercise 36

*Speaker One*

| Examiner: | Let's firstly consider the recent development of a city you know well. |
| Candidate: | Mm. |
| Examiner: | To what extent was this development a result of planning, do you think? |

| | | |
|---|---|---|
| Candidate: | | Mm, I think to some contents, to some extistense. For example, um, the city I live in – Guangzhou – yeah, I feel years ago is, is, um, I think is a city late of planned so you can see, you can find traffic jams everywhere and the buildings are, there are a lot of different types of buildings: the tall buildings, the short buildings and they compress together. And they feel quite uncomfortable why things so many different types of building. Um, the road, the road, I think the transport, transportation system is not so good because late or planned. Um, there so is always traffic jams everywhere. But nowadays there, because the government pay more attention to planned city, now they began to ch …, um, the situation, became better and better … |
| Examiner: | | Okay, okay. Um, let's talk about transport within cities now. Um, what are the different ways people move around a city that you know well? |
| Candidate: | | Well, um, I think in Australia. Um, I think people there away by cars, yeah. That's quite different from our, our country and my city. Yeah, because Aus … Australian people, most of them own cars and they need them to sell them, then take the bus or train to around. Most of them by cars. |
| *Speaker Two* | Examiner: | How important is planning in guiding the development of a city? |
| | Candidate: | Guiding? |
| | Examiner: | Guiding or, or, guiding or shaping the development in a city? |
| | Candidate: | Shaping? |
| | Examiner: | Yeah. |
| | Candidate: | Oh, use guiding or shaping, you say the green, the chairs, like chairs? |
| | Examiner: | Um, more the development in a city. |
| | Candidate: | Um, like, like shilly? |
| | Examiner: | Um, yes, maybe, maybe I'll ask a different question. What do you think large cities will be like in the future? |
| | Candidate: | Large city, ah, in the future? Oh. |
| | Examiner: | Will they be more or less planned? |
| | Candidate: | I, I think, I think if, um, large cities, if I just saying in China, ah, in the future. I think, I think no chairs, no green because, ah, in China the pop … population is very big, have a larger, large number of population so they must have to building, building a lot of house, apartment, ah, provide to the people. So I think larger city will become, ah, a lot of building. |
| | Examiner: | Yeah, okay. So um, what sorts of things do you think could be done to protect environment? |
| | Candidate: | I think maybe government may, maybe do something about protect the g … the environment. Um, maybe, ah, when they |

building some house, building some apartment, they put, ah, they ah, accom … accompany some green chair and garden with them. I think, ah, you can improve productions … environment.

## 18 Exercise 37

Candidate: Um, last today I read the newspaper, um, about Europe very angry that Japan copycat the car. At first I very surprised the word 'copy-cat' because I haven't seen this word so I asked my host family about this. And Europe very angry because they produce the car and desi … the shape, colour and, ah, light in front of car. But Japan always copy each part and I think is, is about copyright so but they can not do anything because is not whole of, whole part of the car but is only a little of part. So now. But they very angry about this.

## 19 Exercise 39

Welcome to the phenomenon that is the Convenience Store. First launched in Australia by the *7–11* company in nineteen seventy-seven, these abbreviated supermarkets of the late twentieth century continue to expand at an incredible rate. Once inside, it's the brightness that registers first. An explosion of massed fluorescent tubes assaulting your eyeballs with pure white light. As your eyes gradually adjust, your sense of nutritional balance is next challenged – with sugar or salt the principal ingredient of almost everything around you. Tightly wrapped in plastic, the displayed goods are unified only in their distance from nature. Vegetables and loaves of brown bread are a rarity but artificially modified confectionery and gigantic muffins are ready and waiting for your custom.

## 20 Exercise 40

1 Could you help me with my preparation for the IELTS exam?

2 Could you help me with my preparation for the IELTS exam?

3 Could you help me with my preparation for the IELTS exam?

4 Could you help me with my preparation for the IELTS exam?

5 Could you help me with my preparation for the IELTS exam?

## 21 Exercise 41

King Street, the main street of Newtown, is the place to go for lunch when you're looking for a break from the frenetic pace of shopping. I'd recommend RooBar for its food. It's been established a long time and is undoubtedly the most stylish café on King Street. Their menu is wonderful especially their all day breakfast of eggs, tomato and sausage on bread for only $5.90. What a bargain! Also, for vegetarians, their extensive non-meat menu includes such delights as scrambled tofu or banana bread.

## 22 Exercise 42

1 I am sick of listening to that terrible banging noise.

2 Who's going to the movies tonight?

**3**  What are you doing on the weekend?

**4**  I thought you said you were going to do the washing up.

**5**  Switch on the light. How often do I have to tell you?

**6**  The lecture, given by Professor Adams, was highly entertaining.

**7**  The weather'll be cool and cloudy for the remainder of the week.

**23**

*Speaker One*

### Exercise 43

| | | |
|---|---|---|
| *Speaker One* | Candidate: | Okay, ah. Well, ah, I think it's a notebook which is very important for me. Ah, well, a notebook you can find everywhere, every store. Ah, I have been actually I have two of them, and around four years ago, and I'm still losing them. I use it to write a lot of them, in there, to write my poems and about me. That's the reason because it's very important. It's not … |
| | Examiner: | So if you lost one, would it be very hard to replace? |
| | Candidate: | Yeah, very hard, because it's a lot of work in that notebook, so, yeah, should be very hard. |
| | Examiner: | So is it like a diary as well or mainly poems? |
| | Candidate: | Well, it's not, maybe you can call diary but it's not the typical diary that you say 'today I did this and I met my friends'. It's more, it's more different, like a kind of know you, yourself. So it's more, I don't know, deep. |
| *Speaker Two* | Candidate: | Ah, yeah, ah. (pause) One of my friend told me there is a event ha … ah, happen, ah, in a small country. Er, the prince of the country has just killed his parent for some reason, because some reason. The king and the queen are all been killed by their son and the, at last, the prince suicide. So this event make the little country quite famous in the world at the moment. These things really struck me deeply because I think, as a prince, he must have high status and he don't worry about his future or something else. |

**24**

### Exercise 44

**Example 1:**  I'd like you to meet Geoff, Lynn an(d) Mark.

**Example 2:**  I'd like you to meet Howard, Catherine an(d) Melinda.

**25**

### Exercise 45

**1** Tuesday    **2** Tuesday    **3** Tuesday    **4** Tuesday    **5** Tuesday.

**26**

### Exercise 46

| | |
|---|---|
| Examiner: | Why did you choose this particular course? |
| Candidate: | Um, because, ah, when I was teaching and I thought I should learn something more about the linguistics, and that's why I, I chose this, um, area to study. |
| Examiner: | Mm, what are the most challenging or difficult things about your course? |

Candidate:     Well … I think the most difficult part is the reading part, because um, quite a lot of a new concepts involved in, and ah, that the things I didn't know before. So I think that's the most difficult part for me.

Examiner:      And what will you do when your course finishes?

Candidate:     Um, teaching, I guess. I would go back and I'm still, I'm doing teaching and I will … I would prefer actually, prefer to use the knowledge I learned here, so back to teaching again.

## 27  IELTS PRACTICE TESTS: SPEAKING

### Candidate 1 (11.51 minutes)

Examiner:      Good morning. I'm Clare. Could you tell me your full name, please?

Candidate:     Yes. Ah, my name is Dai Fen.

Examiner:      And what should I call you?

Candidate:     If you don't mind, you can call me Madeleine, that's my English name.

Examiner:      Okay. And could you tell me where you're from?

Candidate:     I'm from Taiwan.

Examiner:      Can I see your ID, please?

Candidate:     Yes, here it is.

Examiner:      Yes, that's fine. Let's talk about your study or work. Are you currently studying or do you work?

Candidate:     Ah, when I'm studying I'm a applied linguistic student.

Examiner:      Ah hah, and why did you choose this particular course?

Candidate:     Um, because, ah, when I was teaching and I thought I should learn something more about the linguistics, and that's why I, I chose this, um, area to study.

Examiner:      Mm, what are the most challenging or difficult things about your course?

Candidate:     Well, I think the most difficult part is the reading part, because um, quite a lot of a new concepts involved in, and ah, that the things I didn't know before. So I think that's the most difficult part for me.

Examiner:      And what will you do when your course finishes?

Candidate:     Um, teaching, I guess. I would go back and I'm still, I'm doing teaching and I will … I would prefer actually, prefer to use the knowledge I learned here, so back to teaching again.

Examiner:      Mm. Now, let's move on to talk about learning languages. What do you say you are good at speaking … sorry. Would you say you are good at speaking other languages?

| | |
|---|---|
| Candidate: | Mm, not really, I don't think so. |
| Examiner: | Ah hah. Why do you think some people are better at learning languages than other people? |
| Candidate: | Um, possibly because they're, the needs. I mean, people, some people, they are more interested in other cultures – then they had the motivation to learn the other languages. Then possibly that's the reason they are a better speakers than the others. |
| Examiner: | Mm. Are some second languages easier to learn than other second languages? |
| Candidate: | Ah, I don't know. I have tried to learn French but that is very difficult for me. And English, because I have been learning English for quite a long time, so English is – for me – it's easier than French. If I put them to compare together. |
| Examiner: | Mm. What do you think is the most effective way to learn a language? |
| Candidate: | To practise, to use it, to – yep, just to use it, um, with the people from that language, from that culture. I think that's the best way. |
| Examiner: | Let's talk a little about your country. Have you travelled around it much? |
| Candidate: | Not really, I have been to um, some cities but not that much. |
| Examiner: | What's the most popular region in your country for overseas tourists? |
| Candidate: | Mm, I think there are two spots. One is a city called Taitung which is located in the eastern part of Taiwan. Another part, it's called Kenting, is in the northern part of Taiwan. |
| Examiner: | And why is it so popular? |
| Candidate: | Um, I think because those two – okay, for example, like Taitung is um, the city hasn't been developed too much. It's still quite natural, so … and also people are really, really kind there. And less … um, people like um, to go hiking because there is mountains, quite a lot of mountains and the oceans. So they can do … the tourist, the tourist can do many different activities there. |
| Examiner: | Does the government encourage tourism to your country? |
| Candidate: | I think so. |
| Examiner: | How does it do this? |
| Candidate: | They probably just put a commercial in other countries, I don't know. But um, I also know that our government tried to encourage our people to travel around in our own country. That's what I know. |
| Examiner: | Mm. Now I'm going to give you a topic and I'd like you to talk about it for one to two minutes. |
| Candidate: | Mm. |

| Examiner: | Before you talk, you have one minute to think about what you're going to say. You can make some notes if you wish. Do you understand? |
|---|---|
| Candidate: | Yes. |
| Examiner: | Here's the topic and here's a pen and some paper to make notes. |
| Candidate: | Yes. |
| Examiner: | I'd like you to describe somewhere that you have enjoyed living. |
| Candidate: | Mm. |
| | (SILENCE) |
| Examiner: | Okay. Remember you have one to two minutes for this. |
| Candidate: | Yes. |
| Examiner: | I'll stop you when the time is up. Can you start speaking now. please? |
| Candidate: | Yes. Um, the place that I have enjoyed living is called Armidale. It's um, in Australia. It is actually about eight hours away from Sydney and um, it's a very small town. Um, the reason I like Armidale is because they got … Armidale got a different face, let me put it in this way, in every season. Like, in Spring we can see the different types of flowers along the street and Summer is very, very green. And it's not that hot, as well. It's not as hot as Sydney. And my favourite season is in the Autumn because of the trees. And I heard from my friends that those trees are originally from England. And that's why the university there, called the University of New England, I think. And um, the winter – it's quite cold, I would say, compared with my country. Um, but seldom snow. Actually, I haven't seen snow there yet. |
| | Also, it's a very conven … although there is no many um, shopping centres there but I would say it's very convenient for me if I want to do any, any kind of shopping there. Also, what else, mm? |
| Examiner: | Would you go back to live there again? |
| Candidate: | Probably not. I don't think that's a very good place for doing business and the most people live there are students from other countries and also from other cities from Australia. |
| Examiner: | Okay. We've been talking about places where people live. I'd like now to discuss one or two general questions relating to this topic. |
| Candidate: | Yes. |
| Examiner: | Firstly, ah, let's consider the recent development of a city you know well. To what extent was this development a result of planning? |
| Candidate: | Ah, okay. This one is a little bit difficult. I will try, if I can put it this way. The city I know, I would like to use the example of um, the capital city that I'm coming from, Taipei. |
| Examiner: | Mm. |

**Candidate:** The government has ah, planning to build the city of Taipei as one of the international city. So the government have been putting quite a lot of the public transportation, for example. Um, so, and also knocking down some old buildings and they put quite a lot of parks. And ah, some very big shopping centres, for example, as well.

**Examiner:** Do you think the importance of um ... What do you think is the importance of planning, um, in shaping development in urban areas?

**Candidate:** I think that gives, um, if a place is designed well, that it, it will help that each individual areas with a different functions, so we won't mix like residential areas with the commercial area. That won't be a good idea.

**Examiner:** And do you think large cities will become more or less planned in the future?

**Candidate:** I think they will become more planned and actually that is one of the needs that people actually want, because I think more and more people want to doing their business in their commercial area. And when they want to relax, when they want to enjoy their family life, they don't want to hear some, like, a commercial, you know, like announcement all the time, the people are doing business or they will put very loud music. I think they would just like enjoy their own family life in the com ... residential area.

**Examiner:** Mm. We've seen the development of a lot of communities called 'gated communities' recently, which are guarded by private companies and um, you don ... it restricts the entry to non-residents so only residents can go in. Why do you think people choose to live in these kind of communities?

**Candidate:** Um, gated community. Ah, just let me check if I got the idea right? Does that mean the people live in the area, then there's a main entrance that everyone they, they want to go in and leave, they have to go through that main gate?

**Examiner:** That's right, yes.

**Candidate:** All right. Um, I think security probably the major reason. Ah, so if people who choose to live in the gated community, they plobably, plobably (oh, sorry, I have the problem with that word). They perhaps, the reason for them to choose is for the concern of security, as I just say earlier. Ah, they were think that um, some people, if they want to pass or go into the community, they would have to pass some, some guard or things like that.

**Examiner:** Mm. And what kind of people do you think would choose to live in these gated communities?

**Candidate:** Rich people?

**Examiner:** Mm.

| | |
|---|---|
| Candidate: | And if I know, maybe I'm not completely correct. But in my country the people who choose to live in a gated community, usually they are quite rich. And they also require more protection, I think. |
| Examiner: | Okay. Well, thank you very much. That's the end of the speaking test. |
| Candidate: | All right. Thank you. |
| | (INTERVIEW ENDS) |

**Candidate 2 (14.50 minutes)**

| | |
|---|---|
| Examiner: | Good morning. I'm Michael. |
| Candidate: | Good morning. My name is Sato. |
| Examiner: | Okay. Could you tell me your full name, please? |
| Candidate: | Yep, my name is Tatria Sato. |
| Examiner: | Okay, can you tell me where you're from? |
| Candidate: | I'm from Japan. Ah, my home town is Kyoto City. |
| Examiner: | Okay. Can I see your ID, please? |
| Candidate: | Here it is. |
| Examiner: | Thank you. Okay. Let's talk about your study or work. Are you currently studying or do you work? |
| Candidate: | Oh, I'm studying English and I'm not work, working now. |
| Examiner: | Mm. Okay. Um, so just English? |
| Candidate: | Yes, so far I'm studying just English, to could help myself, to, to go to university. |
| Examiner: | Okay. Um, so what about, what are the most challenging or difficult things about um, studying English? |
| Candidate: | Ah, specially, you know, I'm, I studied English for more than ten years in Japan but it's very difficult to speak English. Pronunciation is very challenging for me. |
| Examiner: | Okay, well, what do you think you'll do when your English course finishes? |
| Candidate: | Ah, fortunately I've got unconditional offer from the Master of Accounting course in Macquarie University. So, ah, I've stud ... ah, studying accounting from the 28th of January 2002. |
| Examiner: | Okay. Now let's move on to talk about, um, learning languages. |
| Candidate: | Yes. |
| Examiner: | Would you say you are good at speaking other languages? |
| Candidate: | Ah, pardon me? |
| Examiner: | Would you say you are good at speaking other languages? |
| Candidate: | Sorry, ah, in other words? |

| | |
|---|---|
| Examiner: | Okay. Ah, are you good at speaking other languages? Such as … |
| Candidate: | Ah, other than Japanese? |
| Examiner: | Mm … |
| Candidate: | Mm, to speaking I'm not so good student, yeah, but for reading and writing I have a confidence to do that. |
| Examiner: | Okay. Why do you think some people are better at learning languages than other people? |
| Candidate: | Maybe they're the good student has something talent, you know, and open mind. I think so. |
| Examiner: | Okay. Are some second languages easier to learn than other second languages? |
| Candidate: | Yeah, second? |
| Examiner: | Are some second languages easier to learn than other second languages? |
| Candidate: | Oh, I mean, other than English or something? |
| Examiner: | Mm. |
| Candidate: | Yeah, maybe. Chinese, I have learned Chinese in my univ … Japanese university for three years. It's very easy to read and pronounce because I know the Chinese letter. |
| Examiner: | Yeah. Okay. What do you think is the most effective way to learn a language? |
| Candidate: | Mm, maybe to have friend, ah, who is native speaker, is very effective. And my friend, who has, um, ah, native girlfriend or boyfriend, he's always good speaker. |
| Examiner: | Ah hm. Let's talk a little about your country. Have you travelled around it much? |
| Candidate: | Yes, because I was, I used to be a tour, ah, tour leader in Japan so I, I travelled much, yeah. |
| Examiner: | Okay. What's the most popular region in your country for an overseas tourist? |
| Candidate: | Ah, it's definitely Kyoto, it's my, my home town, that has many temples and shrine, traditional buildings. Mm, very beautiful, yeah. |
| Examiner: | Mm, why is it so popular? |
| Candidate: | Because I, ah, as I said, there are many temples and traditional buildings. So, and also it has nature. |
| Examiner: | Mm. |
| Candidate: | Yeah, much nature, you know. |
| Examiner: | Okay. Does the government encourage tourism in your country? |
| Candidate: | I'm not sure about that. |
| Examiner: | Not sure about that? |

| | |
|---|---|
| Candidate: | Yeah, sure, yes. |
| Examiner: | Okay. Now I'm going to give you a topic and I'd like you to talk about it for one to two minutes. |
| Candidate: | Yes, okay. |
| Examiner: | Before you talk about it you have one minute to think about what you're going to say and you can make some notes if you wish. Do you understand? |
| Candidate: | Yes, I can. |
| Examiner: | Okay, so here's the topic and here's a pen and some paper for you to make some notes. |
| | *(SILENCE)* |
| Examiner: | Okay. Remember you have one to two minutes for this. I'll stop you when the time is up. Can you start speaking now, please. |
| Candidate: | Yes. Ah, the place that I, ah, I have enjoyed living is, um, Kyoto City. I grew up and, ah, I, so, ah. I went to the university in Kyoto and it was very fine. Ah, Kyoto is a very popular city for foreigners but I think Kyoto is a, has another as … aspect, so it is a city of students. Kyoto has many school, high school and especially universities, so I was attending one of these universities. And Kyoto has a lot of, um, entertaining place and a, and the cheap restaurants, as well as the very traditional temples or shrines. So I didn't go any, any temples or shrines though, but I enjoyed living, to living, to live Kyoto. So, um … |
| Examiner: | Do you think it's, um, still much the same place now or has it changed? |
| Candidate: | Mm, I, I don't think, ah, it's changed. It's always a city for stu … many students. It has very, as I said, it has, there are many cheap restaurants. |
| Examiner: | Okay, okay. We've been talking about places where people live. I'd like now to discuss one or two general questions relating to this topic. Ah, let's first consider the design of modern cities. Can you describe the recent development of a city that you know well? |
| Candidate: | Recent development? Let me see. Okay. Ah, when I, when I visit United States it was very modern, modern city, and ah, and was very, you know, in Japan it's very, the city is very messy. So the airport is always entrance for the foreigners but ah, in Japan the access to the airport is very hard, ah, unconvenient. |
| Examiner: | Ah hah. |
| Candidate: | But in United States, ah, it different. So ah … |
| Examiner: | So to what extent do you think the development of these two cities was a result of planning? How would you compare them? |
| Candidate: | Yes, maybe, ah. Mm, United States is not so old country and it was, the city has been developed, ah, for, for within one hundred years or so. Or something. |

| Examiner: | Mm. Yeah. Okay. |
|---|---|
| Candidate: | And it was planned to, to be comfortable for the people. |
| Examiner: | Okay, yeah. How important is planning in shaping development in cities? |
| Candidate: | Cities? Mm, maybe like Australia, ah, there are m …, if there are many natures, trees, it be a very comfortable for the people who are living. And, mm, also we need big street, yeah, and, ah, that, ah, good access to the downtown area. |
| Examiner: | Okay. What do you, what do you think large cities will be like in the future? Will they be more planned or less planned? |
| Candidate: | Less planned? |
| Examiner: | Yeah. Will there be more planning or less planning in cities in the future? |
| Candidate: | Ah, it's … maybe more planning is necessary for the future cities. Mm, I don't know how to, how should, how they should plan to the city but, mm, planning is always necessary. |
| Examiner: | Okay. Um, now, onto another topic here. Um, transport within cities. Think of a city that you know well and what are some of the different ways peoples move, people move about in this city? |
| Candidate: | Yeah, so, in my home country many people use train or buses. Not the same, we may use train to commute or to go somewhere else. And to use car is, ah, limited, you know. We have less car park and to have own car is very, ah, costly. |
| Examiner: | So how many families have cars? |
| Candidate: | Maybe, ah, most of, most families have cars but they can't, they can't use as they want because very, lot, lot of, you know, amusement facility has very expensive car park also. |
| Examiner: | Mm. Okay. In what day, way does a good system of public transportation affect the quality of life for city dwellers? |
| Candidate: | Yeah. Public. Mm, public transportation? For the public buses I sometimes very confused to, how to use the buses and which bus is going which, ah, which place, you know. And so, how to pay a fee is different from the each cities. It's very confusing. |
| Examiner: | Okay. All right. How do you think people will travel round cities in the next century? |
| Candidate: | Next century, yes. Ah, yes, maybe, ah, to go abroad is very common, I think, to become common. And ah, so, the air fee, airplane fees will be, will be very cheap. And so that every, everyone can go overseas. Yeah. |
| Examiner: | Okay. Thank you very much. That's the end of the speaking test. |
| Candidate: | Thank you very much. |

*(INTERVIEW ENDS)*

# Answer key

## Unit 1: LISTENING

**Example page 5**

1 B   2 A   3 laptop (a laptop computer)   4 word processing

5 more expensive   6 lightest   7 2.4   8 most powerful   9 floppy

10 microphone   11 M   12 T   13 TB   14 C   15 A   16 B

**Exercise 1**

1 tomorrow   2 a reason   it was interesting and she learnt a lot

3 a percentage  52%   4 a number  3 (three)

5 a part of the assignment  the references

**Exercise 2**

*Sample answers*

1  At <u>what time</u> did the <u>robbery</u> take place?

2  What is the <u>name</u> of the <u>bank</u> which was robbed?

3  <u>How many customers</u> were in the <u>bank</u> at the time of the robbery?

4  <u>How many people</u> were involved in <u>robbing</u> the bank?

5  What <u>telephone number</u> should people call to <u>give information</u>?

*Answers*

1 9 (nine) o'clock (9am)   2 Central Bank   3 none (zero; no customers)

4 3 (three)   5 9357799

**Exercise 3**

*Answers*

3a listen for (i) type of visa and (ii) duration of visa

3b A

**Exercise 4**

1 ten (10) pages   2 methodology   3 11th September   4 a title page

**Exercise 5**

1 SA233   2 21st January   3 three   4 near the window

5 22 kilos   6 pay extra   7 yes

**Exercise 6**

1 deactivated   2 go out   3 change code   4 fault check

**Exercise 7**

1 C   2 B   3 A   4 B

**Exercise 8**

1 M and J   2 A and J

**Exercise 9**

Check tapescript.

**Exercise 10**

The <u>last</u> decade of the <u>twentieth</u> <u>century</u> witnessed an <u>explosion</u> of <u>interest</u> in the field of <u>travel</u> <u>writing</u>. <u>Bookshops</u> that <u>once</u> only had shelves stocked with <u>atlases</u>, <u>guidebooks</u> and <u>maps</u> <u>now</u> include sections devoted to <u>narrative</u> and other <u>personal</u> accounts of <u>travel</u>. So <u>why</u> the massive <u>growth</u> in <u>this</u> <u>type</u> of travel writing? <u>Some</u> would give <u>credit</u> to a number of <u>authors</u> who have <u>re-invigorated</u> travel writing, with <u>readers</u> enthusiastically <u>responding</u> to their <u>entertaining</u> and often <u>humorous</u> <u>style</u>. But to <u>my</u> mind, the <u>main</u> <u>aim</u> of travel writing is to <u>break</u> the <u>barrier</u> of <u>print</u> and <u>time</u> and to make <u>destinations</u> <u>alive</u> in the <u>mind</u> of the <u>reader</u>.

**Exercise 11**

So, I ask again, <u>why</u> this growth in travel writing? Is it because of these <u>wonderful</u> <u>authors</u> who have re-invented a <u>tired</u> genre? Or is it <u>another</u> reason? <u>I</u> would explain the popularity of the <u>new</u> travel writing as caused by the ever-expanding <u>sameness</u> and <u>uniformity</u> of the world. Nowadays, people find it <u>harder</u> and <u>harder</u> even to <u>find</u>, let alone <u>travel</u> to unusual places <u>themselves</u>, so they want to read about <u>others</u> doing it. Or, if the writing is about a <u>familiar</u>

   FOCUSING ON IELTS: LISTENING AND SPEAKING SKILLS

place, they may want to read <u>how</u> it's been given a <u>new</u> or <u>unusual</u> <u>twist</u> by a talented author.

Comment on focus stress in the above passage:

**why** – rhetorical question to re-focus listener on main subject

**wonderful authors** – ironic use of 'wonderful' (the speaker may not think they're so talented)

**tired** genre – more irony

**another** reason – setting up the speaker's main point which follows

**I** – emphasises that this is a personal point of view

**new** – as a contrast to old and tired.

**sameness** and **uniformity** – speaker's main point, so strong focus stress

**harder** and **harder** – repetition used to exaggerate difficulty

**find** and **travel** – contrast between the two concepts

**themselves** and **others** – contrast between the two concepts

**familiar** – in contrast to unusual places previously

**how** – focus on the content of the writing

**new or unusual twist** – contrast with familiar place/well-known knowledge

**Exercise 12**

Good morning class. Today, I'd like to talk about producing educational multimedia. This particular type of multimedia – as distinct from entertainment multimedia – is an area of interest for educators everywhere. I'd particularly like to discuss the process of producing this type of multimedia. Your first consideration, apart from deciding what medium you're going to deliver your product through, is your audience. Who they are, what they expect and, most importantly, what they need. After you have determined this basic information about your users, then you can go on to the all important area of content.

**Exercise 13**   1 I   2 I   3 I   4 C   5 I   6 C

**Exercise 14**
*Sample answer*

Words worth learning because they are powerful: *local*, *apparently*, *reasonable*, *annual*, *by and large*

Words worth learning because they are of specific use for IELTS: *tutor*, *workload*, *vacation*, *colleges*

Words probably not worth learning: *molecular*

**Exercise 15**
*Sample answers*

| 2 | man: | fellow, guy, chap | 5 | big: | large, huge, enormous |
| 3 | good: | great, terrific, fantastic | 6 | to reduce: | lower, decrease, lessen |
| 4 | bad: | awful, horrible, terrible | | | |

**Exercise 16**

2   a children's doctor           5   a plant/vine with yellow flowers

3   songs in advertisements       6   strong; can survive well

4   a crime

Exercise 17    2   insistent/forceful

two people discussing going to a concert

come on/how about this?/how about that?/I'll pay

persuading/trying to convince someone

*Sample answers*    3   calm/matter-of-fact

two people discussing a machine, possibly in an office supplies shop

it's four machines in one/it's guaranteed/how much does it cost?

describing/demonstrating

4   calm/matter-of-fact/she sounds as if she is talking to an audience

perhaps reading the news on television or on radio

described as/contact the police hotline/today's highlights in sport ...

describing/explaining

5   calm/curious

two people talking about a property advertised for sale

property for sale/just wanted to check/what does that mean?/it simply means/I see

asking for information/clarifying

Exercise 18    2 G    3 C    4 B    5 E    6 A    7 F    8 E    9 D    10 E    11 B
12 F    13 E    14 C

Exercise 19    3   list/describe (the types)

4   request/ ask permission (eg to close the window)

5   list/describe (the advantages)

6   describe (the details)/provide further detail

7   describe the main topic of the lecture/presentation

Exercise 21

|  | | Conversations | | | | | |
|---|---|---|---|---|---|---|---|
| **What the speakers are doing** | | 1 | 2 | 3 | 4 | 5 | 6 |
| asking for information | | ✓ | ✓ | | | | |
| giving information | | ✓ | ✓ | | | | ✓ |
| thanking | | ✓ | | | | | ✓ |
| asking an opinion | | | | ✓ | ✓ | | |
| expressing an opinion | | | | ✓ | ✓ | | |
| agreeing | | | ✓ | | ✓ | | |
| offering/inviting | | ✓ | | | | | ✓ |
| expressing surprise | | | ✓ | | | | |
| reassuring someone | | | | | | ✓ | |

Exercise 22    2 asking for information    3 requesting    4 giving advice    5 arguing

6 declining    7 reassuring    8 describing    9 inviting    10 insisting

**Exercise 23**   1 010306977   2 Smithies   3 Smithers   4 Jacqueline
5 17A Heeley St., Clapham SW11   6 12th August   7 30th September
8 hardanger   9 Liebke   10 1989   11 30th September
12 09.30 (half past nine; nine thirty)   13 7 (seven) o'clock
14 8.30 (eight thirty; half past eight)   15 Axel

**Exercise 24**   1 Conditioning   2 Milling   **3 and** 4 Rollers   5 White   6 Sacking

**Exercise 25**   1 aneroid   2 liquid   3 lever   4 spindle   5 dial

**Exercise 26**   1 C   2 C   3 C   4 C   5 E

**Exercise 27**   1 round   2 long and thin   3 940   4 576   5 96   6 4
7 1797   8 1814

**Exercise 28**   2 (1) Technical   (2) Computer Literacy   (3) Mathematics
3 (1) textbooks   (2) fiction   (3) poems
4 (1) interpreting   (2) simultaneous   (3) consecutive
5 (1) emu   (2) varieties   (3) features

**Exercise 29**   1
*Sample answers*

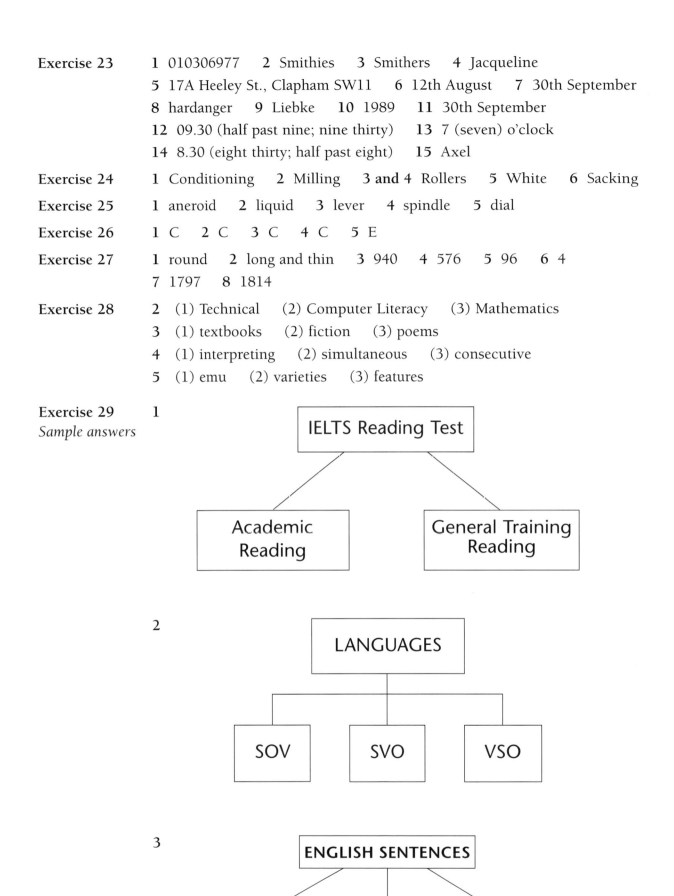

| Exercise 30 | 1 M and D  2 T and J |
| Exercise 31 | 1 Agree  2 Disagree  3 Agree  4 Disagree  5 Disagree |

## IELTS PRACTICE TESTS: LISTENING

### Section 1

1 beautiful  2 ✓  3 ✓  4 very small  5 ✓  6 not enough

7 three  8 half past five  9 0418 327704  10 Eric Bana

### Section 2

11 Head of Security  12 laboratory  13 staff card  14 security officer

15 quickly  16 Purpose of visit  17 Date  18 Time in  19 A  20 A

### Section 3

21 B  22 C  23 A  24 A  25 C  26 B  27 C

28 second-hand  29 Martin  30 money

### Section 4

31 some  32 second  33 culture shock  34 essays  35 invisible

36 less  37 C D  38 A F  39 B  40 D G

## UNIT 2: SPEAKING

| | |
|---|---|
| **Exercise 1** | **Subject area – Your home** |
| *Sample questions* | Can you tell me something about your home-town? Is it a historic place? What's the population? Does it have many attractive buildings? What are the main industries there? |
| *Sample answers* | I come from Sydney. My city is just over two hundred years old and has a population of just over four million people. It has many attractive buildings – the older ones are made of the local yellow sandstone and the newer ones are glass and metal. Sydney's main industries include services, such as transport, tourism and some light manufacturing. |

**Subject Area – Your job/studies**

| | |
|---|---|
| *Sample questions* | What is your occupation? How long have you been in your job? |
| | What are you studying? Do you enjoy it? |
| *Sample answers* | I am a vet and have been one for sixteen years. |
| | I am studying to become a mechanical engineer. I mostly enjoy it, but hate the end of semester exams. |

**Exercise 2**     **Note:** It is NOT ADVISABLE to memorise these questions and answers as it is extremely unlikely that you would be asked these exact questions in the IELTS Speaking Test.

**Your daily routine**

Q: What time do you usually go to work?

A: I usually leave for work just after eight.

Q: How does the weather affect your daily routine?

B: It doesn't really affect it at all, unless it's raining. Then I catch the bus to work instead of walking.

**Leisure/free time**

A: What do you normally do on the days that you don't work?

Q: Not much, I usually just sit around at home and relax.

A: Do you have a hobby that you do every day?

Q: Yes, I read every night for twenty minutes before I go to sleep.

**Accommodation**

A: How many rooms does your current accommodation have?

Q: It's only got four – a bedroom, living room, a kitchen and a bathroom.

A: What do you see when you look out of the windows of your accommodation?

Q: I can see the tops of some trees and the upper floors of a hotel across the road.

**Learning languages**

A: What is the most difficult thing about learning English?

Q: The large vocabulary is difficult to learn – also articles and prepositions are impossible!

A: What other languages would you like to learn? Why?

Q: I'd like to learn Spanish. I think it's supposed to be the world's third or fourth most popular language

**Food and drink**

Q: What do you usually eat for breakfast?

A: I usually grab a bowl of cereal and toast.

Q: How much water do you drink every day?

A: Not enough really. Probably about three glasses.

**Visiting your country/Visitors to your country**

Q: What country do most visitors to your country come from?

A: They come from all around the world, but I think Europeans would have to be the most common visitors.

Q: Are there any places in your country that you wouldn't recommend a visitor to your country to go? Why?

A: I wouldn't recommend the north-west of my country. It's heavily industrialised and the environment has been terribly degraded.

Exercise 3

| General subject area | Exact question asked by examiner | Answer clear and related to question? |
|---|---|---|
| **1** Job/Study | Are you currently studying or do you work? | Yes |
| **2** Study | And why did you choose this particular course? | Yes |
| **3** | And what are the most challenging or difficult things about your course of study? | No (see below) |
| **4** | And what do you think you'll do when your course finishes? | Yes |
| **5** Learning languages | Would you say you are good at speaking other languages? | No (see below) |
| **6** | Why do you think some people are better at learning languages than other people? | Yes |
| **7** | And do you think some second languages are easier to learn than other second languages? | Yes |
| **8** | What do you think is the most effective way to learn a language? | Yes |
| **9** Visiting her country (China) | Let's talk a little about your country. Have you travelled around it much? | Yes |
| **10** | What's the most popular region in your country for overseas tourists? | No (see below) |
| **11** | Is there a particular city that's um, that's popular for tourists? | Yes |

Question 3    The question asks about her course but she appears to focus on difficulties in the workplace

**Question 5**  She talks a little off-topic – her response is about learning languages in general, whereas the question asks her about her personal experience.

**Question 10**  Her difficulties with this question appear to be related to vocabulary.

**Exercise 5**

**Comments on use of linking words**

The candidate uses *and*, *because*, *but* and *so*. A wider variety of linking words could have been used in this presentation but these few words perform adequately in expanding the candidates' ideas.

**Comments on structure**

In the first sentence, the candidate paraphrases the question she has been asked. After this she addresses all the different points on her topic card.

**Exercise 6**  **Topic 1**

*Sample answer*  The city I would like to visit is Rome, the capital of Italy. It's a city that has always attracted me because of its culture. I'm particularly interested in its architecture since it has examples from all major European styles of building. Besides, it was the capital of the Roman Empire, so it has a wonderful collection of public buildings from that time. What I think is great about Rome is that many of the beautiful and historic buildings are still in use – as galleries, public offices and even houses. They are not all locked up as museums. It's really living history there.

Even though it's an expensive city to stay, I'd like to go there for at least a month because there's so much to see and do. Therefore, I'd need to take a lot of money and be careful that I didn't spend too much on Roman food! I'd find a cheap *pensione* – sort of a low budget hotel. It would probably be in the centro storico, the old centre of the city, probably within walking distance of the River Tevere.

Most visitors to Rome would agree that it is a very special place. But for me, it's Europe's most historic and romantic city. While cities like Paris, Vienna and Madrid are lovely too, I think Rome beats them all.

**Exercise 7**  2 C    3 G    4 A    5 B    6 E    7 D    8 F

**Exercise 8**  2  Are changes to food production methods that increase the quantity of food
*Sample answer*       produced always positive?

No, changes in food production methods can also have negative effects. As an example, in this country mass produced food generally doesn't taste as good as naturally grown food. I also worry about the increased amount of chemicals farmers have to use to make sure their soil produces bumper crops. I often wonder if we are eating these chemicals too.

3  Compare the types of food consumed in your grandparents' time to the types of food you consume now.

Well, fifty or sixty years ago, my grandparents' generation had a much more limited diet. They ate what was grown locally, what was in season and little else. In addition, most things they ate were fresh as they didn't have very effective refrigeration techniques. Nowadays, we have a huge variety of food to choose from and we can keep it for as long as we like because of the invention of freezing technology.

4   How will shopping for food change/evolve in the next few decades?

Actually, patterns of food shopping are changing now. A lot of people are starting to buy food over the Internet because it saves time and energy. Also, gigantic supermarkets – called 'hypermarkets' – are springing up on the edges of large cities. Buying food at these places is cheaper as they buy in bulk and pass savings on to their customers, so they are becoming very popular.

**Exercise 9**

*Speaker One*

### Asking for clarification

Are you asking me about a city planning?

So ah, you mean that what do I think about …

Ah, ah, it's … it's very challenging question but I'm not so sure the word that, that you ask me. Ah, the 'gated community', is that mean the um, private property?

Ah hah, yes. Um, you ask me whether this is good for people to live there or what?

### Was she successful?

In the first example, the speaker puts two parts of the question together and makes a more specific question to ask back to the examiner ('Are you asking me about a city planning?') This skill of simplifying the question in your own words is a useful and much used technique in all types of interview situations. She then forces the interviewer to ask the question again, but in a slightly different way (So ah, you mean that what do I think about …?)

In the second example, she again checks her understanding of the main topic by asking a specific question about gated communities ('is [does] that mean the um, private property?'). She then seeks clarification about what aspect of the topic she is being asked about ('Um, you ask me whether this is good for people to live there or what?').

The candidate seeks clarification about questions she is unsure of in a highly appropriate way.

*Speaker Two*

### Asking for clarification

Planning?

You mean, the city plan, planning of city?

The 'influence' – can you explain what is this?

### Was he successful?

This speaker also uses clarification strategies, but not as smoothly as Speaker 1. When he comes up against a difficult topic, he tends to repeat the word he doesn't know. In the first example, the word is planning ('Planning?'). However, he does continue to try to clarify the word by putting it into context and formulating a question to the examiner ('You mean, the city plan, planning of city?'). This is a successful clarification strategy. Unfortunately, the second example is not so successful. Again he repeats the difficult word ('The influence?'), but then asks the examiner to define the word ('Can you explain what is this?'). Asking for an explanation gives a poor impression of your vocabulary abilities – it would be better to guess the meaning and then check that you have the correct meaning. For example, 'Is influence the same as effect?'

| | |
|---|---|
| **Exercise 10** | **Thinking time strategies** |
| *Speaker One* | Recent development? Let me see. Okay. |

So ah …

Yes, maybe, ah.

Cities?

And, mm,

Less planned?

Ah, it's …

Mm,

Yeah, so,

Maybe, ah,

Yeah. Public. Mm, public transportation?

Next century, yes.

**Was he successful?**

In general, this speaker is not very successful in this area. He uses thinking time techniques/fillers, but they are limited to repeating parts of the questions he has been asked ('Recent development?', 'Less planned?') or simple words or sounds ('maybe', 'ah', 'yeah'). Other fillers are sometimes unsuccessful because they are inappropriate regarding register and function. For example, he answers 'Maybe' to the question 'How many families have cars?' His choice of fillers also makes him seem unsure of how to proceed with his response rather than just filling in silent periods.

*Speaker Two*   Ah, okay. This one is a little bit difficult. I will try, if I can put it this way.

Um, so,

And ah,

I think

I think

Um, gated community.

All right. Um,

**Was she successful?**

Speaker 2 is a confident and effective speaker who successfully uses thinking time techniques/fillers when she needs to. She uses a useful thinking time technique when answering the first question by directly addressing the difficulty of the question ('This one is a little bit difficult. I will try, if I can put it this way.'). This gives her enough time to think of a satisfactory extended answer. She repeats part of a question once ('gated community') and uses 'I think' several times when answering the question on planning. She uses a limited variety of 'sound' fillers – her favourites appear to be 'um' and 'mm'.

| | | |
|---|---|---|
| **Exercise 12** | 2 | A few years ago my father reached the age when people stop working. |
| *Sample answers* | 3 | In my spare time I do unpaid work to help people. |
| | 4 | This dish is really good for your health. |
| | 5 | She handed in her assignment on time. |
| | 6 | There are many good reasons for teaching young children foreign languages. |

7   Many people argue that television has a negative effect on children, but the evidence does not clearly prove or disprove this argument.

8   Many people have strongly criticised the government's decision to change the law without discussing it with the public.

**Exercise 13**
*Speaker One*

This candidate does not speak fluently. She hesitates a lot and uses 'um' and 'ah' too frequently. She also repeats words quite often (for example, 'Um, we are all, we all say, ah Cantonese' and 'I, I can, I can eat, I can eat cheaply and I can ah, bought many things ...'). Her overall delivery is very jerky (stop-start) rather than smooth.

*Speaker Two*

This speaker is somewhat more fluent. Although there are repetitions ('I, when I arrived Australian I, I rent ...') and some hesitations ('Ah, it's bed, it has two bedrooms ...'), overall these do not interfere with listening as seriously as the first speaker.

**Exercise 14**

Listen to your recording and assess your own fluency.

**Exercise 15**
*Sample answers*

2   Yes, I have. I've read it already.

3   No, I haven't. I've never been there.

4   No, we don't. We don't have any ferries.

5   Yes, there is. There's quite a lot of crime.

**Exercise 16**
*Sample answers*

2   No, I don't think so. I don't think they should.

3   Yes, I do. I think they should.

4   No, I don't think so. I don't think they will.

5   Yes, I think so. I think it should.

**Exercise 17**
*Sample answers*

2   I liked them. They were really nice.

3   I hate it. The weather's terrible and everything is really expensive.

4   I really like them. They're fun and they help me forget about my study.

5   I like them. They're really convenient.

6   I hated it. It seemed so difficult.

**Exercise 18**
*Sample answers*

3   It's very widespread. I think the majority of people use it at least once a week.

4   They're not that common, actually. I think people still find them too expensive.

5   It plays a huge role. I don't think people could do without it in their lives.

6   It's extremely important. I don't think children know enough about the dangers of drugs.

7   They're very popular. I'd say that 90% of the films we watch come from America.

8   To a limited extent, I think. Some degree of censorship is justified if it is in the interest of national security.

**Exercise 19**
*Speaker One*

This answer is not very coherent. Although there is a direct response ('it is very important'), this does not come at the beginning. It would be better to front this answer (ie bring it to the beginning of the sentence). The point about transportation (which is then repeated) distracts the listener from clearly hearing the answer. Coherence is also damaged when the speaker states that 'the spirit' is very important (whereas the question asks how important *planning* is). If the speaker feels that (encouraging) people's spirit is more important than planning, then that is a valid response, but it needs to be stated very explicitly.

**Speaker Two**     This is a coherent answer. The first words ('possibly because') link directly to the question. She reinforces this by later saying 'possibly that's the reason'. She then repeats the words in the question (but makes a slight error introducing the unnecessary 'a'). The listener clearly understands the opinion she gives in response to the question.

**Exercise 20**     Check your answers with a partner.

**Exercise 21**     2  Yes, I (most) certainly do.
*Sample answers*          Yes, I'm definitely in favour of that.

3  Yes, we have a huge amount of crime.
   Yes, our crime rate is shocking/terrible/appalling.

4  It's enormous and extremely stylish.
   It's really spacious and very attractive.

5  I believe it should be illegal/forbidden.
   It shouldn't be allowed, in my opinion.

**Exercise 22**     3  There are so many. In fact, my home-town is famous for its restaurants.
*Sample answers*     4  I doubt it. I imagine that children will continue to go to school.

5  Yes, I do, actually. The grammar and pronunciation are more difficult.
   Absolutely. It's much harder than other tests I've experienced.

6  Yes, definitely. I think it's much harder. The subjects are more difficult and you have a lot more individual responsibility.
   Yes, it is, actually. Although you have greater responsibility, you also have more freedom.

7  No, there aren't that many really, and outside the big cities there are very few.
   It's the same with them. They're not at all common.

8  No, I don't think so. In my experience children learn languages far more quickly.
   No, not really. As far as I can see, men and women are about equal.

9  Well, it's rather cold but it's extremely beautiful, and the people are very friendly.
   The northern part of the country is hot and dry, and maybe it's not as attractive as the south, but the food is wonderful.

10  Yes, I most certainly do. It makes all children equal regardless of their background.
    Definitely. It's important that they feel equal, and I think it's also good for discipline.

**Exercise 23**     Through the vocabulary which this speaker uses we get a richer picture of the
*Speaker One*     city ('popular', 'foreigners', 'entertaining place', 'traditional', 'temples or shrines', 'cheap restaurants', 'another aspect') and of the person's experience in that city ('grew up', 'was attending', 'enjoyed'). This speaker also demonstrates slightly

more diversity in qualifiers ('many' 'a lot of', 'especially'). Overall, this speaker shows a slightly greater range of vocabulary than Speaker Two.

*Speaker Two*　There is some repetition which indicates a lack of fluency, uncertainty about what to say next, and perhaps a lack of preparedness. Even allowing for this, the vocabulary range is quite limited. The candidate wants to expand on or elaborate on 'economic open market' but only manages a near-repetition 'open economic marketer'. Her qualifying adverbs are limited to one, namely 'very' (for example: '*very* freedom', '*very* lucky', '*very* beautiful' 'not *very* high', '*very* like'). Using other qualifiers such as 'really', 'extremely', 'quite', 'reasonably', and so on, would demonstrate a more diverse range. She occasionally uses related words side by side, but these seem to reflect lexical uncertainty ('living style, standard' and 'alone, just myself'), rather than a demonstration of lexical range.

*Exercise 24*　This speaker has difficulty expressing her meaning ('Internet is, is not so far – govern') and then hesitates. She declares her difficulty ('I don't know how to say') but does not attempt to paraphrase. Perhaps her meaning is that the Internet is not as controlled (monitored/regulated) as TV news.

*Exercise 25*　2　People who have a strong desire to do something are generally more successful.

*Sample answers*　3　I really feel that countries should work together more. If we don't, then the world's climate will get much hotter.

4　I couldn't finish my assignment in time so I asked if I could hand it in late.

5　I think you can trust newspaper reports more than news reports on television.

*Exercise 26*　Listen to the recording of your own presentation and assess you ability to use vocabulary effectively in terms of accuracy, appropriateness and range.

*Exercise 27*
*Speaker One*　This candidate has more frequent and arguably more serious grammatical errors. There are errors in the grammar associated with verbs, for example 'many places that I have been visited' and ' that I have um, enjoy living in over there' and in the grammar associated with nouns, for example, 'first, ah, first reasons', 'one of the place', 'located ah, northern part of Thailand', 'for foreigner', and 'to do some my research'. The past tense is managed successfully ('I went', 'I had', and 'Province was') but no complex grammatical structures are successfully achieved.

*Speaker Two*　This candidate has more accurate grammar. Although there certainly are inaccuracies (for example, 'they got' instead of 'they've got' and 'is green' instead of 'it is green'), the candidate successfully controls complex grammatical structures, including more difficult tenses ('I haven't seen snow there yet'), comparisons ('it's not as hot as Sydney' and 'it's quite cold, I would say, compared with my country'), and multiple-clause sentences ('the place that I have enjoyed living is called Armidale', and 'the reason I like Armidale is because they got ...').

**Presentations with grammar corrected**

*Speaker One*　Yes, um. Where is the place that I have enjoyed living? Um, there are many places that I have visited and Sukhothai Province is one of the places that I have um, enjoyed living in. Ah, there are many reasons why I like to live (*or* I like living) there. The first, ah, first reason is its environment and its surroundings. The second reason is that the people there are really nice and friendly. Thirdly, Sukhothai Province is located not far from Bangkok where I live. It is ... it is about five hundred kilometres from Bangkok and it is located ah, in the northern part of Thailand. Ah, Sukhothai Province, um, was the (location of the?) first um, dynasty ah, of Thailand. So there are many, many historical sites there, so that (or with the result that) Sukhothai is a very popular place for (or with) foreigners. Secondly, ah, I liked Sukhothai because um, I met many friendly people there. For example, I went to Sukhothai five years ago (for five years?) to do some research (or to do some of my research), to collect the data (connected?) with religious (matters?) in, in a village in Sukhothai. Over that period of time (or during that time) I had a lot of good experiences with the, with people there.

| Speaker Two | Yes. Um, the place that I have enjoyed living is called Armidale. It's um in Australia. It is actually about eight hours away from Sydney and um, it's a very small town. Um, the reason I like Armidale is because it has … Armidale has a different face, let me put it this way, in every season. For example, in spring we can see the different types of flowers along the street and in summer it is very, very green. And it's not that hot, as well. It's not as hot as Sydney. And my favourite season is the autumn because of the trees. And I heard from my friends that those trees are originally from England. And that's why the university there is called the University of New England, I think. And um, the winter – it's quite cold, I would say, compared with my country. Um, but it doesn't snow. Actually, I haven't seen snow there yet. |
|---|---|

Also, it's a very conven … although there are not many um, shopping centres there, I would say it's very convenient for me if I want to do any, any kind of shopping there. Also, what else, mm?

| Exercise 28 | 1 | **Comment:** *Your answer should contain verbs in the past tense. It may contain the form used to + infinitive to describe regular past activity. After verbs such as 'like' and 'enjoy' the gerund ('-ing' form) should be used.* |
|---|---|---|
| Sample answer | | I used to play tennis every weekend, and sometimes I used to go hiking. And I always enjoyed watching television and listening to music. |
| | 2 | **Comment:** *The verbs in your answer should be in the past tense. Your answer should include an accurate comparative form. To give an extended answer you should include a reason/explanation.* |
| Sample answer | | I found secondary school far more enjoyable than primary school because we had more sport. |
| | 3 | **Comment:** *Since the question is about (types of) movies in general, your answer should refer to the plural form 'movies'. Again, to give an extended answer you should include a reason.* |
| Sample answer | | I like action movies best because they're really exciting and help you forget about the real world. |
| | 4 | **Comment:** *You need to get the comparative form correct and make sure that you are talking about (plural) 'men' and 'women'.* |
| Sample answer | | I think women are better drivers than men because they concentrate more. |
| | 5 | **Comment:** *To describe regular behaviour the verbs need to be in simple present tense.* |
| Sample answer | | We visit our relatives and eat a very large dinner. Sometimes we sing songs. |

6 **Comment:** *The verbs need to be in simple past tense. You need to know the irregular past tense forms of verbs such as 'feel'.*

*Sample answer*      I had mixed feelings. I was happy to finish, of course, but at the same time I felt sad saying goodbye to all my classmates.

7 **Comment:** *The verbs need to be in present perfect tense, like the question, but if you give information about when or where it happened, the tense changes to simple past tense. Again you need to know the irregular past tense forms of common verbs such as 'take'.*

*Sample answer*      I've never taken the TOEFL, but I took the IELTS last year. I took it when I was in Toronto.

8 **Comment:** *The answer requires the so-called 'second' conditional form.*

*Sample answer*      If I won the lottery, I would give some money to my parents and to charity, and I'd keep the rest in the bank for myself. And I would definitely give up working!

9 **Comment:** *The answer uses the same verb as the question ('was'). In giving a reason for your choice the verbs need to be in past tense.*

*Sample answer*      My favourite teacher at high school was Mr Yamamoto because he was so kind. He really cared about us and used to explain everything so patiently.

10 **Comment:** *As with number 7 above, the verbs should be in present perfect tense, except if you give information about where and when this happened, in which case you use simple past tense. As always, it's important to articulate the plural ending of the noun 'countries'.*

*Sample answer*      I've been to three foreign countries so far in my life. I've been to New Zealand and Australia, and last year I went to Malaysia.

11 **Comment:** *The answer will probably use simple present tense (although other tenses are also possible). Be careful to use the '-s' ending on present tense verbs. It is also, of course, essential to get basic pronoun forms correct ('he/his/him' or 'she/her/her').*

*Sample answer*      My best friend's name is Max. He's about the same age as me, but he's already married, and he has three children! He's a social worker and he really loves his job. We met at high school, so we've known each other for about ten years now. He's a great guy.

12 **Comment:** *The answer should contain accurate comparative forms.*

*Sample answer*      I've always found British English a bit easier than American English. I suppose that's because all of the foreign teachers at our school came from Britain, and I'm more familiar with British pronunciation and idioms.

13 **Comment:** *The answer should contain would + infinitive conditional form (If you use the short form 'I'd', make certain that you distinguish the pronunciation from 'I').*

*Sample answer*      I would tell her (him) to save her money, study hard, and have a plan. And I would advise her to invite her old friends to visit her overseas!

14 **Comment:** *The answer should echo the (present perfect continuous) tense of the question. Make sure that you pluralise 'years'.*

*Sample answer*      I've been studying English for about ten years now. I started in high school.

**15 Comment:** *It is essential that you accurately control the existential there ('be') form, in this case 'there are'. Again, make certain that the noun 'universities' is clearly plural.*

*Sample answer*    There are about 20 universities, I think.

**16 Comment:** *The answer typically requires a simple present tense verb to describe regular behaviour. Make certain that you make 'hours' plural.*

*Sample answer*    I usually sleep about eight hours a day, but lately I've been sleeping only about five hours a day because I've been so busy.

**17 Comment:** *The description will contain simple present verbs but also past tense or present perfect if talking about the history of the building. Passive forms of the verbs may be necessary to describe the building. If you use the structure 'one of the …', remember that it is used with a plural form of the noun.*

*Sample answer*    One of the most famous buildings in my country is the Su Temple. It's a huge building and it's completely covered in gold leaf, so it really shines beautifully in the sunlight. I think it was built about 500 years ago – it's certainly very old. I'm not quite sure who built it, to be honest.

**18 Comment:** *The full answer should contain the verb 'is' and the preposition 'on'. You should use one of the standard ways of describing dates. The description of what you do will probably contain simple present tense verbs.*

*Sample answer*    My birthday is on the twenty ninth of June. (My birthday is June 29th.) I usually just go out with a few friends and have a nice meal.

**19 Comment:** *The answer must contain suggestions: the easiest structure to control is 'I think they should go …' but other forms (with advise/suggest/recommend) are possible. It is likely that the answer will need to contain superlative forms, for example 'the most beautiful'.*

*Sample answer*    I think all visitors should see the north-eastern region of the country. In my opinion it's the most beautiful part of the country and the most interesting in terms of culture. I would advise people to spend at least a week there.

**20 Comment:** *To speculate about the future, the future tense will probably be necessary. Modal auxiliary verbs such as 'might' can also help speculate.*

*Sample answer*    I think so. I think cash will probably disappear completely. We might all just use plastic cards instead.

**Exercise 29**
*Sample answers*

2   He was raised by his grandmother because he was abadoned by his parents (had been abandoned by)

3   He worked part-time after school because he was poor (because he and his grandmother were poor).

4   He was 15 when he left school. (He left school at [the age of] 15.)

5   He has published two novels.

6   Yes, he has. (He has published some short stories).

7   He earned it by selling the film rights to his novel *Eternity*.

8   He won it in 1993.

9   He married Elizabeth Charles.

**10** He was 28 when he got married. He got married at (the age of) 28.

**11** He has (got) two daughters.

**12** Clara is older than May.

**13** He lives (resides) in Monaco.

**14** He is writing a collection of short stories about his childhood.

**15** He doesn't have (any) siblings. (He doesn't have any. He has no siblings. He has none. He hasn't got any. He's got no siblings. He's got none.)

**Biographical description**

*Sample answer*

Francis James Hatton was born in Newcastle in 1967 and had no brothers or sisters. His parents abandoned him when he was very young and he was raised by his grandmother. She was extremely poor so Hatton had to work part-time after school. When he was 15 he left school and went to work in a department store. He left the store in 1987, the same year that his short story 'Black Morning' was published. In the following year he had three more short stories published, and three years after that he quit work to write full time. In 1988 his novel *This Man* was published and two years later he published another novel, *Eternity*. In 1991 he sold the film rights to *Eternity* for 1.5 million dollars and in 1993 the film won an Academy Award for Best Screenplay. In 1995 he married Elizabeth Charles. They have three children, a daughter Clara who was born in 1997, a son Andrew born in 1998, and a daughter May born in 2000. He lives in Monaco now and is writing a collection of short stories about his childhood.

**Exercise 30**
*Sample answer*

**2** This driver's licence belongs to Alicia Maria Murdoch. She lives at 23 Stafford Road, Elizabeth Bay 2011. The number of her licence is 37822AF. She was born on the twenty seventh of June 1966 (June twenty seventh 1966). (Her date of birth is …) The licence will expire on the eighteenth of July 2009 (July eighteenth 2009).

*Sample answer*

**3** This television usually costs $1,999, but now it is reduced (has been reduced) to $1,500. It has a three-year guarantee. (It is guaranteed for three years.)

*Sample answer*

**4** His full name is M Andreas Lopez (His surname is Lopez and his given names are …) He is Australian. (His nationality is Australian. He is an Australian national.) He was born on the eighth of June 1971 (June eighth 1971). His passport number is EF129748. The passport was issued in Sydney on the sixteenth of August 1999 (August sixteenth 1999). It will expire on the sixteenth of August 2009. (The passport's date of expiry is …) The passport is signed by the holder. (The passport contains the holder's signature.)

*Sample answer*

**5** The title of this book is *Thailand*. (This book is entitled *Thailand*). The sub-title is *A handbook in intercultural communication*. (The book is sub-titled …). It was written by Kerry O'Sullivan and Songphorn Tajaroensuk. (The authors are …). It was published by the National Centre for English Language Teaching and Research. (The publisher is …). This book is the fourth in the Language and Culture series.

**Exercise 31**
*Sample answers*

**2** I enjoy living in a small town and I have no desire to move to a big city. I enjoy living in a small town because there is less pollution and crime.

I enjoy living in a small town which is famous throughout my country for its beautiful gardens.

I enjoy living in a small town even though it is more difficult to find work there.

*Sample answers* 3 I think we should reduce the number of cars in our cities and encourage people to use public transport.

I think we should reduce the number of cars in our cities because the pollution is damaging our children's health.

I think we should reduce the number of cars in our cities which are steadily being suffocated by the pollution from vehicle emissions.

I think we should reduce the number of cars in our cities although I realise it will not be easy to do.

*Sample answers* 4 I have never used the Internet and I don't own a mobile phone.

I have never used the Internet because I don't have access to a computer.

I have never used the Internet, which is very unusual for a person of my age.

I have never used the Internet but I'm going to do a computer course next week.

*Sample answers* 5 We need to focus on improving the health of our children and we must also consider their spiritual well-being.

We need to focus on improving the health of our children because they are the future of our community.

We need to focus on improving the health of our children who are, after all, our greatest asset.

We need to focus on improving the health of our children but we mustn't neglect our own health in the process.

**Exercise 32**  1 I've been studying English since I started secondary school about ten years ago.

*Sample answers*  2 I'd like to study at a foreign university so that I can get a better job here at home.

3 It's quite small but it's very comfortable and extremely convenient.

4 I really love speaking English though sometimes it's rather tiring and difficult.

5 I like people who don't take life too seriously.

6 I feel very strongly that people should be able to access a university education without paying.

7 As far as I know men usually get married when they're about 28.

8 They take English because it's the international language and they can get a better job.

9 I try to read it every day but sometimes I just don't have enough time.

10 I'm doing it so that I can get into university.

11 It's hard to know which friend I would choose as my 'best friend' but I suppose it would be Lee. He comes from the same town as me. I've known him for about twenty years, since we studied together in primary school. In fact, we sat side by side throughout primary school and we used to help each other with our schoolwork. Although he went to a different high school and university, we still stayed in touch and remained good friends. When we

were teenagers, we were in the same local football club. We're even closer nowadays because our wives have become really good friends. The four of us often go out together. Lee is a wonderful person. He's kind, considerate, and generous, and he's got a great sense of humour. I really like people who make me laugh. That's probably the main reason he's my best friend.

12 One film I really enjoyed watching was *Gandhi*. I guess it came out about 10 or 15 years ago but I remember that I went to see it about five times. It's about Mahatma Gandhi who of course was one of the leaders of India back in the 1930s, I think it was. It shows the period in India before it became independent. It's quite a long film with a lot of detail and different characters but I never got bored watching it. I suppose I liked it because it was so interesting and because the actor who played Gandhi was so good. Also it really showed me that you can achieve things peacefully. I always enjoy films that make me think.

**Exercise 33**
*Speaker One*

This candidate uses reasonably complex structures. Although there are some inaccuracies, she shows a clear command of compound sentences ('my father gave me this four years ago and it is the most important thing …') and of complex sentences, including those with clauses of reason ('because I can think of my day', 'not only because of this disease'), condition ('if I can call like this'), contrast ('but it's always more comfortable …'), and circumstance ('I don't depend on anyone when I want to go out').

*Speaker Two*

This candidate's mastery of more complex structures seems limited to compound sentences ('Yeah, it's apartment on the floor sec … on the second floor and um, it is on the corner of the Fontenoy Road and the Lane Cove Road'), and complex sentences containing clauses of reason ('because I think, firstly, I can, I live here very comfortable …') and result ('so I'm like my unit very much').

**Exercise 34**
*Sample answer*

Jack was very well dressed and well groomed, but he was also very nervous. He can speak both French and German, but he wasn't able to answer the question about customer complaints. Perhaps he is a little immature. Patrick was also well dressed, but his grooming and posture were poor. He can speak French but his German is rusty. He was able to answer all the questions and he seemed very mature. I'd recommend Patrick because we can help him improve his grooming and posture and his German, whereas we can't easily help Jack become more mature. This position really requires a confident, mature person.

**Exercise 35**

Listen to the recording of your responses and assess your ability to speak accurately and appropriately.

**Exercise 36**
*Speaker One*

This student has generally satisfactory pronunciation, although she needs to slow down and concentrate on producing individual sounds more accurately. She mispronounces a few words such as 'extistense' (extent?), 'sell them' (seldom?) and occasionally chops off some word endings.

*Speaker Two*

This student has below average pronunciation. She often mispronounces individual sounds, uses incorrect word stress and lacks linking and rhythm. In particular, she has problems with words such as shading (shaping), chairs (trees?), shilly (Sydney?) accompany and production (protect?). A native speaker would have some difficulty in understanding parts of this discussion.

**Exercise 37**    This candidate has trouble with producing word endings – many of her words are chopped off – as well as problems with some sounds. Specifically, problems occur in ab<u>out</u> (mispronunciation of diphthong /aʊ/), ca<u>r</u> (missing word ending), a<u>sk</u>ed (mispronunciation of consonant cluster), desi<u>gn</u> (missing word ending), alway<u>s,</u> (missing -s ending) copyri<u>ght</u> (mispronunciation of consonant cluster).

**Exercise 38**    Personalised sound list and practice.

**Exercise 39**    <u>We</u>lcome to the phe<u>no</u>menon that is the Con<u>ve</u>nience Store. First <u>launch</u>ed in Australia by the *7–11* <u>com</u>pany in <u>nine</u>teen <u>se</u>venty-<u>se</u>ven, these abb<u>re</u>viated <u>su</u>permarkets of the late <u>twen</u>tieth <u>cen</u>tury con<u>tin</u>ue to ex<u>pand</u> at an in<u>cred</u>ible rate. Once in<u>side</u>, it's the <u>bright</u>ness that <u>re</u>gisters first. An ex<u>plo</u>sion of massed fluo<u>res</u>cent tubes as<u>saul</u>ting your <u>eye</u>balls with pure white light. As your eyes <u>grad</u>ually ad<u>just</u>, your sense of nu<u>tri</u>tional <u>bal</u>ance is next <u>chal</u>lenged – with <u>su</u>gar or salt the <u>prin</u>cipal in<u>gred</u>ient of <u>al</u>most <u>eve</u>rything a<u>round</u> you. <u>Tight</u>ly wrapped in <u>plas</u>tic, the dis<u>played</u> goods are <u>u</u>nified <u>on</u>ly in their <u>dis</u>tance from <u>na</u>ture. <u>Ve</u>getables and <u>loaves</u> of brown bread are a <u>rar</u>ity but artif<u>ic</u>ially <u>mod</u>ified con<u>fect</u>ionery and gi<u>gan</u>tic <u>muf</u>fins are <u>rea</u>dy and <u>wait</u>ing for your <u>cus</u>tom.

**Exercise 40**    1    The speaker wants to focus on the listener as a possible provider of help.

2    The speaker wants to focus on him/herself as the person needing the help.

3    The speaker wants to focus on the IELTS exam as the particular exam he/she needs help with.

4    The speaker wants to focus on the preparation for the IELTS exam as the particular type of help needed.

5    The speaker wants to focus on the particular aspect of IELTS for which help is needed.

**Exercise 41**    **King** Street, the main street of **Newtown**, is **the** place to go for **lunch** when you're looking for a **break** from the frenetic pace of **shopping**. I'd recommend **RooBar** for its **food**. It's been established a **long** time and is undoubtedly the most **stylish café** on King Street. Their menu is **wonderful** especially their **all day breakfast** of eggs, tomato and sausage on bread for only **$5.90**. What a **bargain**! Also, for **vegetarians**, their extensive **non-meat** menu includes such delights as scrambled **tofu** or banana **bread**.

**Note:** All the stressed words are content words (ie mostly nouns with a few adjectives)

**Exercise 42**    2    Who͜'s going to the movies tonight?

3    What are you doing on the weekend?

4    I thought you said you were going to do the washing up.

5    Switch on the light. How often do I have to tell you?

6    The lecture, given by Professor Adams, was highly entertaining.

7    The weather'll be cool and cloudy for the remainder of the week.

**Exercise 43**
*Speaker One*    This speaker has a good English rhythm which he has probably transferred from his first language (Spanish). He stresses words differently depending on their importance to the meaning he wants to convey and uses pausing appropriately.

*Speaker Two*  This speaker doesn't use English rhythm in his speech and places equal stress on each word he utters. His speech is notable for uncomfortably long pauses and its inconsistent pace.

**Exercise 44**  Ask your partner to assess your English rhythm.

**Exercise 45**  1 D    2 C    3 B    4 E    5 A

**Exercise 46**  A  **Examiner:**    Mm, what are the most challenging or difficult things about your course?

Candidate:    Well … I think the **most** difficult part is the **reading** part,

because um, quite a lot of a **new** concepts involved in, and ah,

that the things I didn't know before. So I think that's the most

difficult part for me.

**Intonation used:** The speaker shows uncertainty at the beginning of the sentence by an extended fall-rise on the word *well*. (**Function 4**) Other intonation in the sentence follows a standard pattern for the delivery of statements. (**Function 3**)

**Other features:** Sentence stress on **most**, **reading** and **new**. The last sentence is shared (repeated) information, so it is said quickly without stressing.

B  **Examiner:**    And what will you do when your course finishes?

Candidate:    Um, **teaching**, **I guess**. I would go back and I'm **still**, I'm doing

**teaching** and I will I would **prefer** actually, prefer to use the

**knowledge** I learned here, so back to teaching again.

**Intonation used:** The speaker shows she is unsure of her future expectations by use of a fall-rise tone at the beginning (**Function 4**). She shows her strong attitude towards the subject by the use of a rise-fall tone in middle of her answer (**Function 5**) and a falling tone with her repeated statement at the end (**Function 3**).

**Other features:** Highlights **still**, **teaching**, **prefer** and **knowledge** and uses pausing effectively to display some conflict between her goals.

## IELTS practice tests: Speaking

### Assessment of speakers

#### *Candidate 1*

**She speaks quite fluently.**

She speaks at a reasonable pace and in a smooth manner. For example, when she says 'If you don't mind, you can call me Madeleine, that's my English name', her words flow together smoothly and rapidly. Her Part 2 presentation is also fluent: the pace is appropriate, and there are no significant hesitations or breakdowns.

She sometimes pauses when she speaks, but she generally manages to keep these pauses very brief. She 'fills' the pauses with 'um' and 'ah' while she quickly thinks about what she is going to say next. For example: 'Um, because, ah, when I was teaching and I thought I should learn something more about the linguistics, and that's why I, I chose this, um, area to study.'

She uses thinking-time techniques quite well throughout. In one instance, she gains thinking by using 'well' and then echoing (or slightly rephrasing) the question: (Examiner: What are the most challenging or difficult things about your course? Candidate: Well, I think the most difficult part is …) In another instance, she gains time by responding to the question with a long 'mm' filler: 'Mm, not really, I don't think so'. In yet another example, she gains time by making a comment about the question: (Examiner: To what extent was this development a result of planning? Candidate: Ah, okay. This one is a little bit difficult. I will try, if I can put it this way). Throughout the test she gives the impression that she is thinking about what to say next, not that she is stuck (and doesn't know what to say next).

**She speaks very coherently.**

Her answers in Parts 1 and 3 are always relevant to the examiner's questions (eg Examiner: Why do you think some people are better at learning languages than other people? Candidate: Um, possibly because they're, the needs. I mean, people, some people, they are more interested in other cultures – then they had the motivation to learn the other languages. Then possibly that's the reason they are a better speakers than the others.) Everything in the answer relates to the question.

Her answers usually show that she has understood the questions by echoing or rephrasing them. (eg Examiner: And do you think large cities will become more or less planned in the future? Candidate: I think they will become more planned and actually …)

There are instances when her answers relate very coherently because she uses pronouns to refer back to nouns in the questions. (eg Examiner: What do you think is the most effective way to learn a language? Candidate: To practise, to use it, to – yep, just to use it, um, with the people from that language, from that culture).

She generally presents her points in a very clear and logical manner. In the Part 2 presentation, for example, she first clearly presents her topic (Armidale), then describes its location, and then starts to talk about why she enjoyed living there (thus answering the question), giving examples to illustrate her points. This is a coherent presentation of information that is easy for the listener to follow.

**She uses vocabulary effectively.**

Her vocabulary throughout seems accurate and appropriate. There appear to be no instances where she has used the wrong words to express her meaning.

She uses quite a good range of vocabulary. For example, in her answer about Taipei she uses words such as *government*, *build*, *international*, *public transportation*, *knocking down*, *buildings*, *parks*, and *shopping centres*.

She demonstrates a wide repertoire of qualifiers (indicating the extent of something): for example, *very difficult*, *quite a long time*, *some cities*, *a little bit difficult*, *quite a lot of mountains*, *quite natural*, *developed too much*, *more and more people*, *not that much*.

At some other times, the range of vocabulary is a little limited: for example, in Part 3 where she tends to limit herself to *I think* in expressing her opinions.

The words she uses are appropriate for an examination/interview. In the first stage of the interview, for example, she replies with full formal responses such as *yes, my name is …* and *yes, here it is* (and avoids more informal responses such as *yeah* or *sure*). At the end of the test, she uses the appropriate *All right, thank you*.

When confronted with an unfamiliar term, she successfully clarifies the meaning by paraphrasing: Um, gated community. Ah, just let me check if I got the idea right? Does that mean the people live in the area, then there's a main entrance that everyone they, they want to go in and leave, they have to go through that main gate?

**She uses grammar effectively.**

Her grammar is largely accurate. For example, she uses the plural form consistently (in her presentation, she speaks of eight hours, different types of flowers, those trees), though in Part 3 there are a few errors (each individual areas and a different functions). Her use of articles is generally quite accurate; for example, in her question confirming the meaning of 'gated community', all four articles are used correctly. Similarly, she uses comparative and superlative forms of adjectives accurately (eg it's easier than French and the most difficult part), as well as relative clauses (eg I would prefer actually, prefer to use the knowledge I learned here). She also selects tenses accurately and forms them accurately (eg I have been to um, some cities and I have tried to learn French). She uses the verb *to be* correctly (that's my English name) and the existential there (be) (eg there are two spots). She controls adverbs correctly (they probably just put a commercial), and adverbial clauses (I don't think that's a very good place for doing business.)

There are grammatical errors, such as 'the government has ah, planning to build the city of Taipei as one of the international city' and 'the most people live there are students from other countries' but these do not cause any significant difficulty for the listener in following her meaning.

She uses a range of sentence structures, mixing simple sentences (eg That won't be a good idea) with compound and complex sentences (eg It is actually about eight hours away from Sydney and um, it's a very small town; One is a city called Taitung which is located in the eastern part of Taiwan; I also know that our government tried to encourage our people to travel around in our own country; I think they will become more planned and actually that is one of the needs that people actually want, because I think more and more people want to doing their business in their commercial area).

**She speaks quite clearly.**

She speaks loudly enough. The listener does not need to strain to hear what she says. Her production of individual sounds is generally quite accurate and presents no significant difficulties for the listener. There are occasional problems: for example, she sometimes has difficulty in distinguishing 'l' and 'r', so that the 'r' sounds in *probably* and *security* are pronounced as 'l'. Perhaps this is due to the influence of her native language. There are a few other relatively minor problems: for example, the first vowel in 'natural' (*it's still quite natural*) is not accurate.

Her use of word stress is consistently accurate. For example, *community*, *announcement*, *before*, *motivation*, *developed*, and *government* are all pronounced with correct stress.

Her use of sentence stress is generally (though not invariably) successful. For example, in: 'I don't think that's a very good place for doing business and the most people live there are students from other countries and also from other cities from Australia', she stresses *business* and *students*, which is appropriate, but her stress on *cities* does not appear necessary or appropriate. Her use of focus stress can be very effective: for example, in her answer to the examiner's question: 'And do you think large cities will become more or less planned in the future?' she places a focus stress on *more* and thus responds in a very clear manner to the question: 'I think they will become more planned and actually ...'

She links words effectively when she speaks. For example: *Ah, I-don't-know. I have tried-to-learn French but that is very difficult for-me. And English, because I have been learning English for quite-a long time, so English-is, for-me it's-easier than French if I put-them to compare together.* There are many examples of appropriate linking, such as in her Part 2 presentation when she says that the town *is not-as-hot-as-Sydney.*

Because she links effectively, and uses word stress and sentence stress appropriately, she achieves an overall rhythm which is reasonably similar to the rhythm used by native speakers of English.

She uses intonation appropriately to support her communication. For example, when she says 'Rich people?' she uses intonation to present this as a suggestion to be confirmed, and in the sentence 'I have been to um some cities but not that much' she finishes with a falling tone to indicate a completed statement. In turn, when she says 'I think there are two spots' she uses a low-rise tone to indicate incomplete information.

**Overall, this candidate speaks very effectively.**

She clearly knows how to participate in a formal interview and speaks in an appropriately formal manner. Her overall demeanour appears calm and focused. She is particular adept at using clarification strategies, paraphrasing, and 'thinking time' techniques to help her through any difficulties she encounters. This also helps her maintain her fluency throughout the interview. Her communication is also very coherent throughout the test, linking her responses very directly to the questions asked and presenting her points in a clear and logical manner. Her grammar and vocabulary show a reasonable degree of accuracy and range. Throughout, she speaks at a good pace and at an appropriate volume. Her pronunciation is clear. In all, she would most probably receive a score which would enable her to study at postgraduate level in an English-speaking country. The best chance for her to further enhance her score would be to reduce the number of grammatical errors and to broaden her range of vocabulary somewhat.

### Candidate 2

**He does not speak fluently.**

The candidate does not achieve a reasonable pace or smoothness in his spoken delivery. He stops after almost every word or group of words, hesitates, then produces another word or two, hesitates again, and so on. When speaking on a very familiar topic the delivery becomes more fluent (eg Kyoto has many school, high school and especially universities, so I was attending one of these universities. And Kyoto has a lot of, um, entertaining place and a, and the cheap restaurants, as well as the very traditional temples or shrines.) but this fluency easily breaks down, especially when he is uncertain about grammar (eg So I didn't go any, any temples or shrines though, but I enjoyed living, to living, to live Kyoto). The hesitation fillers 'ah' and 'um' are over-used, and do little to help maintain fluency.

His concern for grammatical accuracy disturbs the flow of his communication. Repairing grammar as you speak is natural and does not necessarily impede communication. This candidate, however, does not repair his errors, so much as offer a range of alternatives hoping that one of them will be correct (eg I enjoyed living, to living, to live Kyoto and most of, most families; I don't know how to, how should, how they should plan to the city).

He has some ability to use 'thinking time' techniques, and thus maintain his fluency (eg Yeah; Public; Mm, public transportation? Recent development? Let me see; OK; Ah).

**He does not always speak coherently.**

Occasionally the candidate's answers link very coherently to the questions. For example in the following exchange the answer directly follows the meaning of the question and successfully echoes its tense: Examiner: Do you think it's, um, still much the same place now or has it changed? Candidate: Mm, I, I don't think, ah, it's changed. Another example of correct linking is the answer 'Ah, the place that I, ah, I have enjoyed living is, um, Kyoto City', which follows the tense indicated on the Part 2 card.

Often, however, the grammatical link between answer and question breaks down (eg Examiner: Do you understand? Candidate: Yes, I can.) Sometimes the answer does not relate in meaning to the question; for example, in response to the question about the effect of public transportation on the quality of life, the candidate speaks about difficulties in managing fares and routes. This answer is not relevant. Similarly, the question about the recent development of a city does not receive a relevant coherent answer. Sometimes the link in communication breaks down completely (eg Examiner: Does the government encourage tourism in your country? Candidate: I'm not sure about that. Examiner: Not sure about that? Candidate: Yeah, sure, yes.)

The candidate seldom shows that he has understood the questions by echoing or rephrasing them. (eg Examiner: Are some second languages easier to learn than other second languages? Candidate: Yeah, maybe. Examiner: How important is planning in shaping development in cities? Candidate: Cities? Mm, maybe like Australia ...)

When the candidate *does* successfully understand the question, the content of the answer is generally logical, relevant, and appropriately sequenced. The Part 2 presentation, for example, is reasonably coherent, and the listener can follow the description easily enough.

**His vocabulary is somewhat limited in its accuracy and range.**

The candidate uses vocabulary which is generally accurate and appropriate to the intended meaning. There are some significant errors, however. For example, he uses *air fee, airplane fees* instead of 'fares' or 'airfares' and talks about something being *unconvenient* instead of 'inconvenient'. He could have paraphrased these with 'cost/price/ticket' in the first instance and 'not convenient' in the second. Occasionally his meaning is not clear because of inappropriate word selection, for example *there are many natures*.

He displays some range in his vocabulary, with words such as *commute* and *shrines*, which are precisely appropriate for the intended meaning, and he uses some synonyms such as *abroad/overseas* and *costly/expensive*. More typically, however, the range of vocabulary is quite limited. For example, the answer about planning uses the word *necessary* twice instead of using a range of words. In the answer about English, the echoing of the words *difficult/challenging* may make the answer very coherent, but fails to display any diversity in vocabulary. In qualifying adjectives he almost invariably uses *very*, for example *very confused/confusing/cheap/expensive/costly/comfortable/modern/messy/hard*. In speculating/giving an opinion, he invariably uses *maybe*.

He uses the synonyms *yes/yeah/yep* but in a formal examination/interview these might best be limited to yes. Other expressions used are suitably formal, such as thank you very much.

When uncertain about the meaning of a question (which is relatively often) he uses clarification strategies, with varying degrees of success. As strategies, both *Ah, pardon me?* and *Sorry, ah, in other words?* are acceptable, but there are two other instances which are not accurately formed, namely: *Oh, I mean, other than English or something?* and *Ah, mean other than Japanese?*.

**His grammar is quite limited and often inaccurate.**

There are a number of instances of accurate grammar, especially in simple sentences using present tense (eg Maybe more planning is necessary for the future cities; Planning is always necessary; Pronunciation is very challenging for me.) The simple past tense is also sometimes successful (eg And it was planned to, to be comfortable for the people; I grew up and, ah, I, so, ah; I went to the university in Kyoto and it was very fine). However, both of these tenses often break down (eg Ah, when I work, when I visit United States it was very modern, modern city) and other tenses are also not formed accurately (eg Ah, I've stud …, ah, studying – which should be 'I will study' or 'I will be studying').

Some more challenging structures are successful (eg *confused* and *confusing* are used correctly), but too often there are significant errors in more basic structures (eg Yes, so far I'm studying just English, to could help myself, to, to go to university; So I didn't go any, any temples or shrines (absence of *to*); in United States, ah, it different (absence of the article and verb *to be*); it be a very comfortable for the people (inappropriate form of *be*).

Although there are some attempts to mark number (singular/plural) appropriately, the overall control of number is problematic (eg And my friend, who has, um, ah, native girlfriend or boyfriend, he's always good speaker; So the airport is always entrance for the foreigners but ah, in Japan the access to the airport is very hard, ah, unconvenient). In such cases, the listener cannot readily follow the precise meaning.

The candidate appears to have particular difficulty in expressing quantity/degree, with such consistent errors as *Yeah, much nature* and *I travelled much, yeah* and *the good student has something talent* and *not so old country*.

Grammatical range is limited. Although there are instances of compound sentences (eg We have less car park and to have own car is very, ah, costly) and complex sentences (eg It's very easy to read and pronounce because I know the Chinese letter), it is simple sentences which predominate throughout. Another typical pattern is using a series of simple sentences each commencing with *and*. These do not really constitute compound sentences. (eg Ah, yes, maybe, ah, to go abroad is very common, I think, to become common. And ah, so, the air fee, airplane fees will be, will be very cheap. And so that every, everyone can go overseas. Yeah; Yeah, so, in my home country many people use train or buses. Not the same, we may use train to commute or to go somewhere else. And to use car is, ah, limited, you know).

**He does not always speak clearly.**

The candidate speaks loudly enough and the listener does not generally need to strain to hear what he says.

The production of individual sounds is reasonably accurate and presents no significant problems for the listener. The candidate is able to pronounce sounds which sometimes cause difficulty, for example, the /θ/ sound and sometimes the plural '-s' on nouns.

The use of word stress is generally accurate, with appropriate stress on words such as *fortunately*, *unconditional*, *accounting*, *university*, *confident*, *effective*. Occasionally, the correct word stress is not associated with the necessary reduction of the vowel in the unstressed syllable, for example, *entrance*.

The candidate has difficulty with sentence stress. Although there are instances where sentence stress is placed appropriately and supports the meaning (eg Mm, I, I don't think, ah, it's changed), these tend to be shorter simpler sentences, and

are in the minority. More commonly, sentence stress is unclear or inappropriate. (eg Yeah, so, in my home <u>country</u> many people use train or buses. Not the same, we <u>mainly</u> use train to commute or to go somewhere else.) In the first sentence he places the focus stress on 'country' whereas it should be on 'train' or 'buses' and in the second sentence he places the focus stress on 'mainly' whereas it should be on 'commute' to support the main point of that sentence. There are other examples where misplaced sentence stress makes it hard for the listener to catch the intended meaning (eg So I didn't go any, any temples or shrines though, but I enjoyed living, to living, to live <u>Kyoto</u>). Here the sentence stress is on 'Kyoto', so that the listener is left unsure of the point of the sentence.

Because his delivery is not fluent and because he misplaces sentence stress, the overall rhythm of his speaking is rather different from the rhythm typically used by native speakers of English. The rhythm should help to reveal the speaker's meaning but too often with this candidate it works against meaning.

He often uses intonation appropriately (eg And ah, so, the air fee, airplane fees will be, will be very cheap. And so that every, everyone can go overseas. Yeah). Here the rising intonation on 'overseas' does not indicate that he has finished. To show that he has finished he uses the word 'yeah' instead. There are similar problems throughout (eg Mm, maybe like Australia, ah, there are m …, if there are many natures, trees, it be a very comfortable for the people who are living. And, mm, also we need big street, yeah, and, ah, that, ah, good access to the downtown area). Here the rising intonation on 'living' and 'area' is inappropriate and in both cases the intonation signals that the answer will continue, but it doesn't.

**Overall, this candidate needs to work more on his spoken English.**

This candidate would most likely not achieve an IELTS score sufficient to enter university in an English-speaking country. There are difficulties in all areas judged by IELTS examiners.

The candidate appears somewhat nervous and hesitant. This is sometimes expressed as nervous laughter, especially when he is not sure of the meaning of questions. Further practice speaking in authentic situations as well as in IELTS exercises would help, as would relaxation techniques.

Whether from nervousness or a lack of experience in listening to fluent speakers of English, the candidate has difficulty in understanding the examiner's questions. In addition to extensive listening practice (particularly under test-like conditions), he needs to select appropriate clarification strategies and practise forming and using them accurately in context.

He generally does not relate his answers very directly to the questions. Echoing or rephrasing the question would make his communication more coherent and would also give him some 'thinking time'. Starting the answer with an echo or rephrase of the question might also guide grammatical selections when answering.

The candidate achieves an acceptable volume and produces individual sounds accurately enough, but the lack of fluency means that he does not achieve appropriate sentence stress which in turn affects his rhythm. The listener must make an effort to follow the intended meaning.

In his IELTS study program the candidate should place greater emphasis on developing fluency. When speaking in authentic situations or doing practice exercises, he should focus on speaking fluently and not concern himself too much with the ongoing accuracy of his grammar or vocabulary. In terms of pronunciation, this means that he needs to practise speaking with clearer sentence stress and appropriate intonation. In this way he can improve his overall rhythm, and thus make his English easier to follow. As he becomes more fluent and more confident, he could then gradually pay more attention to reducing errors in grammar, vocabulary and pronunciation. Finally, further practice will then be needed to expand the range of grammatical structures and vocabulary he is capable of using.